KNOWLEDGE WITHOUT EXPERTISE

SUNY Series in Science, Technology, and Sociology
Sal Restivo, editor

KNOWLEDGE WITHOUT EXPERTISE

ON THE STATUS OF SCIENTISTS

By Raphael Sassower

State University of New York Press

Published by
State University of New York Press, Albany

For information, address the State University of New York Press,
State University Plaza, Albany, NY 12246

Production by Christine Lynch
Marketing by Lynne Lekakis

Library of Congress Cataloging-in-Publication Data

Sassower, Raphael.
    Knowledge without expertise:on the status of scientists/by
    Raphael Sassower.
        p.cm. (SUNY series in science, technology, and sociology)
        Includes bibliographical references and index.
        ISBN 0-7914-1481-7 (hard:alk. paper).—ISBN 0-7914-1482-5
    (pbk.:alk. paper)
        1. Knowledge, Sociology of.2. Knowledge, Theory of-
    -Psychological aspects.3. Expertise.4. Social sciences-
    -Methodology.I. Title.II. Series.
    BD175.S27   1993
    306.4'2—dc20   92-22750
                                                        CIP

10 9 8 7 6 5 4 3 2 1

Dedicated to Joske a.k.a. Joseph Agassi

CONTENTS

PREFACE

To speak of knowledge without expertise is at once to problematize the notions of knowledge and expertise. Must knowledge claims be supported by expertise? Is it possible to know without the aid or council of experts? And similarly, what epistemological status is granted to experts and their pronouncements? Are there set criteria by which to demarcate experts from non-experts? Moreover, is it important, for a whole range of issues and circumstances, to bother with the delineation of expertise as a cultural phenomenon whose authority is presumed to have been accepted by society as a whole?

I raise these questions in order to illustrate to what extent my attempt to explore the postmodern notion of expertise is challenging and complex. When these and similar questions are raised about the notion of expertise, they inevitably bring into play an entire host of social factors and historical precedents that impinge on any exploration. In some sense, it is impossible nowadays to carve out an area of research or a specific notion and examine it in isolation from its historical context and related cultural frameworks that condition its formulation. So, in order to contextualize the notion of expertise, I have focused my attention most closely on a discipline, political economy or economics, and tried to understand to what extent its leadership and fellow-workers can be considered experts and to what extent the pronouncements and judgments of economists should be perceived as expert advice.

The choice of what is considered in the academy a social science in order to deal with expertise presupposes a host of debatable issues. First, is there a difference between the sciences (natural and hard, social and soft, behavioral)? If yes, does the choice of economics beg the question of scientific expertise? My sense is that exactly because economics is a field of research fraught with ambiguities as to methods of analysis it would enhance my exploration and allow me to examine on what grounds disciplinary distinctions are made in terms of scientific credibility. Second, is it possible to generalize or make an analogy between whatever I find in the case of political economy and any other field of research or any other group of alleged experts? All generalizations and arguments from analogy ought to remain suspect; yet, this does not preempt my own trial in the sense that its procedures—using a historical case study, for example—may be applied (in part on completely) to other domains of presumed expertise. Third, are knowledge claims necessarily limited to particular disciplinary boundaries? If the answer is yes, then it makes sense to ask questions about expertise within the context of academic disciplines. But of course such a position limits the extent of knowledge claims to those produced in the academy, which, in turn, is obviously too narrow and therefore an untenable position. So, my own choice is that of convenience, where the documented record is accessible and renders a possible deconstruction and reconstruction of what may be meant by the notion of expertise. Finally, are the intertwined notions of knowledge and expertise understood in a uniform sense? As I try to explain here, there are traditional binaries that capture the difference between, say, theoretical and practical knowledge, but which lose their significance in the face of particular circumstances (e.g., how to resolve a strike). Having said that, I must confess that there might be various junctures in this book wherein my loose use of terms will give the impression that I endorse a broad and monolithic definition of concepts and notions. But that is not the case, since my continued effort to tackle the questions I raise here illustrates the difficulties with which I struggle throughout the book and the multiple answers I provide in order to appreciate the complexity of dealing with experts and their advice.

Traditionally, a preface is a dedication to an authority, a Pope, a King, or a benefactor; it is also a sort of confession, a personal account that mitigates whatever is contained in a book. As we read the texts of the history of ideas we quickly recognize that no one could have been fooled by the discrepancy between an author's preface, may it be Descartes or Rousseau, and the biting critique that followed, humbly accepting the authority of the Church while undermining all of its principles and doctrines. In my case, I have three confessions to make. First, this book is published in a series on the sociology of science, but its appeal does not fall so neatly into such a niche: it falls in between many categorical stools, from philosophy to the social sciences, from methodology to sociology and ethics, from science and technology to politics and pedagogy. I must admit that this is a deliberate attempt to defy disciplinary boundaries and conceive of problems as broadly as culturally possible. Second, my orientation can be described as postmodernist, but this description says too much and too little about my technique of analysis. I formulate traditional arguments or deliver flat assertions when they are respectively useful and appropriate; I deconstruct and reconstruct a historical case study but probably highlight issues that historians of science would find marginal; and finally, I speak in my own voice whenever possible so as not to pretend that the voice of objectivity and value-neutrality is rightfully mine. Third, this book draws sporadically, and probably not enough, from contemporary feminist critiques of science. To a certain extent I conceive of this book as a parallel project, a complementary one, but not one that can and even pretends to speak for feminists or pursue their specific agendas. In this light, then, I plead for potential alliances between my work and that of others, the way one hopes to contribute to a larger whole, a broad-based corpus of critiques of the hegemony of the scientific enterprise and its expert leaders.

A postmodern perspective is sometimes accompanied by a variety of disclaimers about the multiplicity of interpretations, the temporal authority of one's judgment, and the impossibility of originality. None of these disclaimers amount to a wholesale condemnation of postmodern projects or to the meaninglessness of anything resembling a postmodern critique. Instead, these disclaimers are encouragements to betray the convictions and the purposes that permeate postmodern critiques. In my case, I think that epistemological questions are intimately connected to psychological factors and concerns so that in order to fully appreciate epistemological debates one needs to contextualize them culturally and at times personally. In the present context, this translates into viewing questions about expertise not exclusively in terms of the methodological debates that I review (in political economy) of the past one hundred years, but also in terms of a recurrent cultural appeal to oracles and scientists as leaders and guides for thought and action. In this respect, then, one must explain *what* one knows and *how* it is known as well as *why* one wants to know a particular thing.

To summarize: I think that epistemological questions are directly linked to psychological factors and conditions so that in order to appreciate a methodological debate one should also examine some broader cultural circumstances and the personalities of those engaged in the debates. As for the purpose of this book, it criticizes certain accepted norms concerning the privileged and esteemed status accorded to experts (primarily as scientists and technicians) not so much for the purpose of discarding them as a group or disregarding everything they have to say. Rather, one goal is to appreciate the use that can be made of expert advice and the extent to which experts ought to be seen as public servants whose role is to provide the best tools and information with which to make public policies. Having said that, one is reminded that this position may be viewed in a postmodern world as yet another idealized and old-fashioned democratic picture whose time has passed. I think it possible to radicalize this position by focusing on the notion of empowerment and a concern with education, realizing that the discussions about expertise are about power relations and the distribution or dissemination of power from established institutions to localized groups of activists (however they define themselves).

Another goal of this book has to do more with the institutionalized organizations of the academy, prompting a revision in the classification of research, and the obliteration of disciplinary boundaries. As fiscal crises continue to haunt establishments of "higher" learning, there will be ample reasons to undermine experiments with inter- and counter-disciplinary bent. My discussion of political economy illustrates the extent to which disciplinary boundaries are difficult to maintain and the extent to which their elasticity enhances potential changes at least within academic circles. In this respect, then, this book addresses philosophers and social scientists alike, anyone who has any interest in science and its privileged position in contemporary society, and those whose lives are affected in one form or another by the reign of expertise amidst the terrors of postmodern civilization.

The chapters of this book are organized in an order that continues to refer back to the first chapter, trying to amplify the issues that are raised there and develop additional concerns about the complex notions of knowledge and expertise, given the division into disciplines. At the same time, each chapter can be read independently from all others as a self-contained capsule or an independent answer to the question about knowledge without expertise. When read together, the chapters of this book provide five different perspectives or viewpoints or interpretations of the same set of issues: the role of experts in contemporary society, the language of expertise, and the process by which individual empowerment can be undertaken within postmodern culture. In this sense, one should feel free to choose a reading order according to one's interests and purposes; my order is suggestive at best.

Chapter 1 reviews what happened to Section F (Political Economy and Statistics) of the British Association for the Advancement of Science (BAAS) around the end of the nineteenth century—the attempt to expel the entire Section from the Association—in order to illustrate how certain scientific experts viewed other scientific experts. The disclaimers and criticisms that were launched across disciplinary boundaries almost one hundred years ago to discredit economists have their echoes in contemporary debates among natural and social scientists, even though no direct references to the 1870s are provided. The difference among the disciplines and their methods of inquiry has been cast as a hierarchy of the sciences, where the natural sciences are "preferred" in some methodological sense to the social sciences. Even when the preference is justified (e.g., given a set of empirical data to be explained), such a preference is not left within the context of methodological debates exclusively or limited to answering a specific set of questions. Instead, once a preference is established it is influenced and in its own turn influences the change of political, social, and economic conditions that surround the activities of scientists in their interaction with the public. One of the purposes of this chapter is to evaluate critically the notions of pristine objectivity and value-neutrality that supposedly accompany scientific debates. As is common with other debates, the stakes here were personal and political, dealing with power relations and the relations established in our culture, using knowledge claims as the weaponry with which to further particular causes or the prestige of a group of researchers.

Though I do not wish to sensationalize this chapter, one could summarize its context—beyond the methodological issues of political economy—in terms of sex, violence, and money, three key ingredients that commodify our culture. Sex has to do here with the suspicion with which women were greeted by scientists outside of Section F, having participated in that section (and that section alone) as audiences and speakers; violence has to do with a strike that members of Section F were able to resolve and for which they were reprimanded by their "pure science" colleagues; and money has to do with the ambivalence about allowing Section F to stay in the BAAS because of the dues its members paid (large percentage of the whole because of the Section's popularity) and the grants received by its members (low percentage compared with members of other sections); in short, it was a profitable Section.

Chapter 2 is concerned with the linkage of epistemology and psychology, between the "objective" knowledge that is produced by a group of experts and those who come in contact with that knowledge as recipients or consumers. To think of knowledge in the abstract is to miss its effects as well as the context of its production. If knowledge is produced to respond to certain social and individual needs, these needs should not be exclusively defined in political and financial terms, because these needs are connected to the immediacy of the personal. The status granted to experts of all sorts, from nuclear scientists, physicians, and lawyers to librarians and car mechanics by society (perhaps inadvertently), licenses experts to dictate to the rest of (non-expert) society how to choose between alternatives and what epistemological parameters should be considered. Since society as a whole is responsible for this licensure, any social or individual frustration with the status and effects of expert knowledge is in fact self-induced and therefore has to be reconsidered and revised.

In this chapter, I use the concept of oracles to illustrate a certain historical continuity between previous generations and their anxieties and our own generation and its confusions. This is not to say that "nothing has changed," but only to reconstruct the privilege of experts in cultural and psychological terms with only scant reliance on the epistemological features on which they ground their status and prestige. This posture does not mean to minimize the import of epistemology or the efficacy of certain scientific methods or techniques, only to put them in a broad cultural perspective.

Chapter 3 reviews the presuppositions most commonly associated with the notion of expertise by considering a postmodern narrative on dichotomies. From Jean-François Lyotard's perspective, the distinction between philosophers and sophists has been accepted in the tradition as a delineation whereby one group (and their method of inquiry and linguistic techniques) is preferred to the other on epistemological grounds. My critical examination of Lyotard's notion of dichotomy and its relation to the notion of hierarchy relates back to disciplinary hierarchies exemplified in the BAAS. I find even Lyotard's postmodern conditioning puzzling in its putative protection of scientific, empirical knowledge from the sorts of critiques launched against other forms of narrative expression. Perhaps a deep-rooted cultural anxiety regarding knowledge (with its explanatory and predictive powers) has to be traced to the myth of expertise as it has been formulated already by Socrates. What turns claims of expertise into myths is the disregard for the subtleties of expert claims in their theoretical and practical guises, so that choices can be made by the public regardless of the presumed authority and continued appeal to experts as oracles.

Chapter 4 pushes the concerns of the first three chapters in its focus on the relation between psychology and economics as two disciplines understood in contemporary culture (i.e., the academy) to be independent of each other. My contention is that they (or, for that matter, any two or three disciplines) can be perceived as being simultaneously intertwined and appealing to a set of criteria by which to classify both natural and moral philosophies. Divorcing knowledge claims from their cultural contexts, whether in psychology or economics, makes sense only if one holds onto the belief that dichotomies necessarily portray a hierarchy and that there is a clear demarcation between expert knowledge and knowledge claims provided by any individual in a society. Otherwise, one must be careful to appreciate the broadest context of one's study so that seemingly tangential and marginal factors and conditions are fully accounted for in the formulation and presentation of one's study.

Chapter 5 is concerned with standard perceptions of how experts should or should not interact with the public. I move this discussion from one level of abstraction—speaking of experts and the public—to another—speaking of the leaderships of different groups. The two extreme views on the matter stipulate complete delegation of authority to experts on the one hand or complete subordination of expert advice to the public's decision processes. I include some remarks about the specific democratic context that informs the ideology of our western culture. A compromise with experts and their leaders has to be radicalized enough so that individual citizens will find themselves not only participating in the process that leads to public policy-making, but also would be empowered by their involvement.

Chapter 6 reconsiders the question of expertise from a multiplicity of perspectives and attempts to push the question of empowerment a step further. It deals with two related issues: the issue of privilege in intellectual and methodological terms, and the issue of the politics of intellectual discourse. If one's goal is intellectual empowerment, then "party lines" should be secondary to the accomplishment of that goal. If one's goal is a critique of the status quo (the hegemony of scientific discourses and institutions), no matter how it is defined, then one should encourage more rather than fewer ways by which these critiques may be undertaken. Finally, if one's goal is to reach as wide an audience as possible, intellectual squabbles that add nothing to the proliferation of ideas and forms of critique should be avoided.

In this chapter, I use the labels of postmodern, feminist, Popperian, and Marxist to capture in a Weberian ideal-typical sense four groups of critics, without fully developing their ideas and differences. I do so deliberately in order to illustrate the complexity of any attempt to bridge the gaps among different critics and their schools of thought. I find it perplexing that critics would vent their frustration more readily against their fellow-critics (even if of a neighboring school) instead of venting them against the dominant group—the establishment or mainstream or the upholders of the status quo. Perhaps the reason for this situation is twofold: the dominant group is too vague to define and therefore does not lend itself to straight forward and categorical attacks, and at the same time other critics are ready-made and easily spotted targets whose agendas are clearly defined and therefore lend themselves more readily to an attack. But this situation would obviously benefit the dominant group and undermine the possibility of altering the status quo or even challenging its authority. In this sense, then, the conflation of different forms of critiques—of science and expertise—shows what could be a more useful way of dealing with experts.

ACKNOWLEDGMENTS

"The Myth of Expertise" has been published in Social Concept (1988a) and "Philosophical Hierarchies and Lyotard's Dichotomies" has been published with Charla Phyllis Ogaz in Philosophy Today (1991). Portions of these essays instructed the writing of chapter 3. "Critical Synthesis on the Interdisciplinary Relations Between Economics and Psychology: Estranged Bedfellows or Fellow Travellers?" has been published in Social Epistemology (1989) and has provided the basis for parts of chapter 4.

I wish to thank the Center for the Arts and Humanities and the Committee on Research and Creative Works at the University of Colorado at Colorado Springs for two generous summer stipends for 1990 and 1992 to pursue research for and complete writing of this book. I am most grateful to Charla Ogaz for her continued criticism of my work in progress and her encouragement to improve its final version. Special thanks go to Cheryl Cole for contextualizing this work into cultural studies proper, and to Louis Cicotello for his input on the cover.

CHAPTER 1

Scientists on Trial:
Section F of the BAAS

I: INTRODUCTION

An interesting story can be told about Section F of the British Association for the Advancement of Science during the 1870s, interesting because of what it tells us about an appeal to scientific authority. The appeal of years past to religion turned, at least since Francis Bacon, into an appeal to the authority of science. But science, like religion, has no appeal whatsoever and no authority without qualified and designated agents. If the agents of religious institutions were oracles and priests as divine intermediaries, their secular counterparts, scientists, are intermediaries with "nature." They all claim to have direct access to "infallible" sources of knowledge regarding the mysteries of "Nature" and/or "God," thereby ensuring their credibility.

Can these agents of power and authority ever be challenged? If yes, must scientists themselves challenge other scientists? What are the stakes—benefits and costs—associated with the challenge of scientists? Is the exercise of challenging these agents worth the price of antagonizing an important group of people? If not, what is the price of keeping this group unchallenged? Once challenged, can scientists ever regain their power and authority, their effectiveness? Is it important that they do?

These questions can be answered in various ways when the story of Section F, one of many sections established over the years in the British Association for the Advancement of Science (BAAS) is recalled. This case clearly illustrates the craving for expert/scientific status—a position of power and authority that is removed from the public because its language is beyond the comprehension of most people—and the continuous challenge, on methodological grounds, by one group of scientists regarding the achievement of such status. Section F includes economics, a relatively young discipline during the 1870s that in its quest for scientific legitimacy provides an interesting example of a methodological debate that was transformed into a debate about the linguistic tools that are deemed appropriate for use in a scientific discourse (using the prestigious language of biology after Darwin, rather than the language of Newtonian physics).

1

II: BACKGROUND

The modern history (since 1776) of political economy has periodically suffered scorn at the hands of those considered "scientists," a label introduced by William Whewell only in 1840. The episode discussed here culminated at the 1877 Meeting of the BAAS. The decade in which this episode unfolded was a transitional one for economics, witnessing the decline of classical economics dominated by Adam Smith's original formulations and the revisions of David Ricardo, and the beginning of the formation of neoclassical economics, which later found its notable expression in Alfred Marshall's works. During that period, there was also a strong challenge by the British historical school undergoing its own *Methodenstreit* vis-à-vis the prevailing standards of the day. What makes the illustration of the 1877 episode most interesting is that though it was partially concerned with methodological questions, the main line of defense for the "legitimacy" and "scientific credibility" of economics was based not only on a specific (and historically relative) view of science, but also on images that were dominant in another field of bona fide scientific inquiry. Moreover, instead of using the standard images of physics, the legitimacy of which was beyond reproach, the defenders of economics used biological images. These images were to recur after J. K. Ingram's Presidential Address of 1877 in Marshall's *Principles* of 1890.

Before reviewing the historical record one may reflect on the appropriateness or the very idea of defending one's field of inquiry on the issue of scientific legitimacy. In a period when one acknowledges that words and idioms, linguistic tools and techniques, are not merely the "representatives" of ideas and methods of inquiry, but instead construct the very methods and ideas they are supposed to re-present, one can no longer merely claim to pay attention to the language of economics, for example, as opposed to the issues that are treated by economics. The two are not separate nor are they two sides of the same coin. Rather, the language of economics *is* economics proper. So, the language with which methodological issues are presented and eventually resolved may "translate" into more or less attractive linguistic images that may convince much more than hundreds of examples of the success of this or that method.

If one is concerned whether or not a linguistic defense is indeed an effective guard against questioning the scientific legitimacy of a field of inquiry, one must also ask: Can an epistemological and methodological dependence on one science, say biology, secure scientific status for another, such as economics? Put differently, can the use of one linguistic imagery as opposed to another secure a shield from public and professional criticism? Is this, in fact, all that is required, namely, a linguistic switch? Economics has habitually resorted to that kind of defense, not recognizing that in doing so it is immediately implicated in the problems plaguing other sciences. As the record of the BAAS shows, other sciences were challenged about their scientific status, having to explain what allowed them to count themselves among the bona fide sciences. So, one may also ask: what specific standards are employed to decide what should and should not count as science? During the 1870s, the standards were those of the Baconian-Newtonian tradition (mixed with the positivism of Comte), endorsed by Harcourt, for example, and articulated (with a revision) by Whewell (more on both later). This view of science remained at the core of the Victorian image of science, a core persisting unscathed well into the twentieth century.

Contemporary discussions of the scientific status of economics can be divided into those taking that status for granted, and those involved in methodological debates which are supposed to safeguard that status regardless of any specific methodology that is or is not in current use. This situation seems not to take into account the historical record of economic theory, a record that can help explain why the field may remain less susceptible to certain images of scientific rigor than, say, physics, and at the same time raise fundamental questions about the very nature of scientific inquiry. In doing so, economists can deflect unwarranted criticisms leveled exclusively at them as well as examine certain issues of philosophical interest which may guide the whole scientific community. That is, as the story of Section F of the BAAS is retold here, the issue at hand is not the scientific status of economics alone but instead the very claim to scientific status whatsoever.

III: THE BRITISH ASSOCIATION FOR THE ADVANCEMENT OF SCIENCE

In 1877 there was an attack on Section F—Statistics and Political Economy—of the BAAS, and in 1878 J. K. Ingram, its President, defended Section F. What led to this attack? What is the historical background that culminated in such a blatant attack? Is there something unique in this moment of the BAAS' history? One can answer these questions using a variety of primary and secondary sources, claiming that some are of greater merit and reveal the "truths" of the situation in question in a more precise manner. However, making a choice about one's sources is itself an interpretive commitment, one that is open to criticism. For example, the present reliance on Jack Morrell and Arnold Thackray (1981) may lead one to a different interpretation and allow one to draw different conclusions than a reliance on Susan Faye Cannon (1978).[1]

In some sense, the formation of the BAAS was a response to the inability of some "Gentlemen of Science," as Morrell and Thackray label them, to reform the dominant scientific establishment of the Royal Society of Science in London. But the establishment of the BAAS was not merely a response to another institution; it was hoped that it would accomplish much more than the formal presentation of scientific discoveries.[2] The hope was to have scientists of different fields of inquiry meet one another and discuss their work, as well as open their discussions to a much wider audience around the "British Empire." One can argue also that the establishment of the BAAS was partly due to the new sense and importance of science in Victorian culture.

The fifty years preceding the first meeting of the BAAS of 1831 were marked by the major achievements of the Industrial Revolution. Factories and mass production replaced older methods of agricultural cultivation, and new industrial centers sprang up around the empire with financial muscle previously reserved only to London. Moreover, the engineers that engendered great technical innovations and carried out the scientific discoveries of the day evolved as a counterbalance to the sanguine academics of Oxford and Cambridge. Social, economic, and even political power was rapidly shifting from the established centers of London, Oxford, and Cambridge to Liverpool, Manchester, and Birmingham. The cultural climate of the time ensured a receptive audience for an organization such as the BAAS.

In addition to disseminating scientific knowledge throughout the empire, the BAAS could also serve a lobbying function, pressing for governmental support of scientific research (Morrell and Thackray 1981, 2–9). Finally, in their comprehensive study of the early years of the BAAS (covering 1831–1845), Morrell and Thackray claim that "the particular genius of the British Association for the Advancement of Science lay in its ability to serve as an instrument of public order and social cohesion while at the same time smoothing over the contradictions and internal tensions that characterized the scientific clerisy ["a national church of the intellect", 20]" (Morrell and Thackray 1981, 22).

The first meeting of the BAAS at York in 1831 had many symbolic messages expressing the orientation of the BAAS: it was away from the traditional centers of academic and scientific inquiry, it was supposed to promote social integration, and it was meant by its organizers to reach out to the general public (Morrell and Thackray 1981, 63). Organizations similar in structure and orientation to the

BAAS—popularizing science while enforcing its importance beyond the scientific domain—were already operating in Switzerland and Germany and can be claimed to have inspired such an enterprise in Britain, yet there were several British modifications that catered to the specific conditions and needs of the empire (Morrell and Thackray 1981, 76).[3] The BAAS, in turn, inspired the formation of the American Association for Advancement of Science in 1848, even though the American version had its own national agenda.[4]

The new sense and importance of science in the Victorian culture is partly due to the establishment of the BAAS. Because it was in the news and captured the imagination of the general public (far beyond the confines of the scientific community) throughout the British Empire, "it came to be seen as the intellectual progenitor of technology, the guarantor of God's order and rule, the proper way of gaining knowledge, and the key to national prosperity and international harmony . . . science became a cultural resource" (Morrell and Thackray 1981, 96). That is, "science"—a set of ideas and methods of inquiry assembled and codified around that time—provided an "orderly" shift from the authority of religious institutions toward a secular scientific framework.

Science, however, was not a mere conduit for transformation, a mediator between the "old" and the "new." Instead, it could also become a cultural resource, or at the very least be perceived as such, because of the efforts undertaken by the gentlemen of science, the leaders of the BAAS. They ensured that there was continuous and sufficient aristocratic patronage, that the growing metropolitan gentry (not confined anymore to London) participated, and they never forgot to retain prominent positions within the BAAS for academics, many of whom were at that time also members of the clergy. The diversity of those involved in one capacity or another distinguished this group from any other of the learned societies which were rapidly being established around Britain (Morrell and Thackray 1981, 124).

How could such diversity be kept under one roof? What common ground did clerics and experimenters find within the edifice of the BAAS? The BAAS attempted to unite a multiplicity of interests in the pursuit of a "transcendental end": truth—knowledge—*scientia*. While separating science from politics and theology to achieve union within and progress of the BAAS, there was also the realization that only by showing that science is a peaceful and desirable resource—one that does not threaten the established authorities but only enhances their power and prosperity—could the leaders of the BAAS claim the political fruits they coveted (Morrell and Thackray 1981, 224, 246–7). A presentation of the peaceful nature of science might have convinced those not involved in science, but would not have satisfied working scientists. To them Harcourt offered the Baconian ideals which the BAAS was expected to fulfill (Morrell and Thackray 1981, 267). More specifically, this vision was part of an ideology of science that eventually informed the modern world of the possibility of establishing an intimate relation between science and industry.[5] So, the BAAS could present itself in any manner suitable to those it attempted to court without losing its "scientific" character.

The founders of the BAAS were surprised at the immediate success of their meetings and the financial strength they garnered without difficulties. The cultural climate outside the BAAS was ripe, the people were eager, and the stage was ready for the performances of scientists. Their "entertainment"—as reports, experimental "feats," and imaginative speculations—had some practical impact on the cities where they performed, not to mention the prestige and notice these cities acquired by the sheer presence of so many eminent scientists from around the nation (and some international guests too).

The professional climate internal to the BAAS, however, seems to have been less open to public scrutiny and quite autocratic. A few gentlemen of science set the rules of the BAAS to guarantee control. Not only did they set the rules, but also they were the only ones in a position to enforce these rules. Nominations rather than elections was the standard procedure, and these nominations ensured that a particular vision and ideology remained intact and could determine the operations of the entire organization. Though it can be argued that the BAAS became as autocratic as the Royal Society, the younger institution (BAAS), still aspiring for national recognition, allowed some external pressures to determine the course it eventually took. The case in point is the formation of Section F.

The history of the formation of Section F—at the beginning known as "Section VI. Statistics" (1833), and later known as "Section F" (1835)—is informative in setting the stage for many controversies, the most striking of which is that of 1877. It was Charles Babbage who was said to have been "the gadfly who stung the Association into admitting a statistical Section." Babbage circumvented the "rule" stipulating that only the General Committee could establish new sections, and presented the then president of the BAAS, Adam Sedgwick, with the formation of the section. Part of the pressure to agree to such a section was the impression made by the foreign visitor Adolphe Quetelet when reporting on his statistical studies on suicide and crime. Besides, both Richard Jones and Thomas Malthus were the invited guests of Whewell, and their presence must have convinced Babbage that his idea for a separate section would be acceptable (Morrell and Thackray 1981, 291).[6]

Sedgwick's only argument against the formation of a Statistical Section was his warning that statisticians should limit their inquiry to numbers and facts, and avoid the controversial social and political topics to which their studies may lead them.[7] Such a warning, of course, made sense to those convinced of the correctness of a certain portrayal of the scientific enterprise, where scientific "research" has nothing to do with the rest of society, where the mutual impact of "science" and "society" is completely overlooked, or where scientific practice is decontextualized. At the meeting in Edinburgh (1834) most of the gentlemen of science were already regretting their permission for the formation of Section F a year earlier, for a controversy erupted there during the discussion of the Poor Law.

Year after year, meeting after meeting, there seemed to be some controversial—that is, social, economic, or political as opposed to "scientific"—issue discussed in Section F. These controversies irritated and agitated notables such as Whewell and Galton to suggest the abolishment of Section F altogether. The aristocratic and clubbish character of the Association was threatened when the topics of discussion came so close to the political and economic turmoil of the day: how was the BAAS to distinguish itself from a trade association? It was neither similar to the House of Commons, where representatives argued policy questions, nor was it similar to an academic institution, where the intelligentsia was insulated from public accountability. As such, the discussions carried on in Section F violated the peaceful image and ideology that was presented to prospective participants and supporters. Is this what science is all about? How, then, does it differ from theology and politics?

One form of retaliation against or show of dissatisfaction with the "unscientific" behavior of Section F was to grant members of the section minimal funds for research; the other was to limit the number of delegates from other statistical societies. In addition, the gentlemen of science at the BAAS took it upon themselves to use their "constitutional right"—a self-proclaimed right—to nominate presidents of that section who would be sensitive to their own views of the "appropriate" nature and scope of statistics (e.g., Sykes for 1841). Finally, the reports of Section F were limited to abstracts, or not even published at all in the official Report of the BAAS (from 1835–1844 only three reports were published).

Why did the BAAS not do away with this problematic section altogether and permanently ensure no future embarrassments? One reason may be that in the early years there had been a continued interest in promoting the BAAS and in ensuring its financial strength and survival. Section F attracted crowds so large that during the 1840 meeting, since the room reserved for it was too small, it had to adjourn to a nearby church (Morrell and Thackray 1981, 293–196, 478). Since audiences paid fees and participants enrolled in the Association for a fee, it seemed prudent to keep the section alive and collect money and at the same time monitor closely its internal affairs. Incidentally, this line of argument on behalf of Section F was also formally forwarded to the Council as a defense when formal charges were launched against the section.[8]

Eventually Section F was called "Statistical Science," and by 1863 it was called "Economic Science and Statistics." An episode of particular interest for my study of knowledge without expertise took place during the meetings of 1877 and 1878, but in order to understand it better a review of the ongoing attacks by some prominent members of the BAAS should precede it. The evolution of Section F from an exclusive focus on "statistics" to the inclusion of "political economy" or "economic science" may itself help explain the origins of the attack on economics. Economics was attacked just as statistics was attacked; both Whewell and Galton were antagonistic toward the statistical studies of their day and were therefore inclined to attack economics, too. Their attacks seem to challenge the epistemological and ontological foundations of both statistics and economics.

But an attack along these lines, as will be shown later, cannot stop at an epistemological or ontological level of discourse. It leads, in one way or another, to a discourse about the nature of science, the activity of scientists, and the validity of any claims they make on behalf of their disciplines. So, if there were a justification for attacking or denouncing Section F as the weakest link in the great chain of British science, it was related to the view of the leaders of the BAAS that the demise or break of that link could bring about the demise of the whole scientific chain and threaten the well-being of the empire.

IV: THE ATTACK BY WHEWELL

Though separated by over forty years, there are certain similarities between William Whewell's attack on statistics and economics in the 1830s and the attack for which Francis Galton was responsible in the 1870s. There are, though, some important differences. Both Whewell and Galton were well versed in the mathematical tools of their day, and therefore found ample "justifications" for rejecting some modes of argumentation and calculation that they disliked. But unlike Galton, Whewell was interested enough in economic issues to contribute to the field.

An indication of Whewell's interest in economics is the fact that he was commissioned to deliver a series of lectures on political economy to none other than the Prince of Wales. Most of the lectures are of no interest here, especially since he quotes extensively from Adam Smith and David Ricardo, and only adds few observations of his own. But his own comments reveal the ambiguity with which Whewell approached his subject-matter.

Concluding his third lecture, he says: "But this part of Political Economy [demand and supply] is not so far advanced in the establishment of general rules, that we can apply mathematical calculation to it with any advantage. To do so would only give a false impression of the certainty and exactness of our results" (Whewell 1862, 52). This statement appears to be in sharp contrast to Whewell's own novel publications on the elasticity of demand (in formal mathematical terms).[9] Whether or not economic problems are susceptible to a "formal" treatment or systematization deserves some attention, for it highlights the continued misunderstanding and confusion of the public in regards to the scientific status of economics, and more generally in regards to the potential for forecasting precise predictions by experts using their scientific research.

The contrast between Whewell's own work and the statements made to the Prince may be mitigated when examining Whewell's view of the methodology of science, a view that is difficult to label or categorize. Whewell's view on the methodology of science was formulated through his historical studies of science and his work on the philosophy of science. Whewell was torn between the Baconian insistence on induction, and the success of scientists like Newton in using the deductive method. In some sense one can call Whewell's own methodology "neo-inductivism."[10] If Whewell's work in economics is considered both inductive and deductive, it does not permit a clear delineation in terms of his methodological preference (Hollander 1983, 131, 133, 140). More precisely, there is an apparent frustration that "the task of deriving the basic principles by induction was so immense that . . . the materials of the social sciences might prove intractable and not allow the construction of the requisite body of a small number of universally valid axioms" (Hollander 1983, 146).

This assessment is in agreement with Whewell's own assertions that it is possible to explain the mistaken views of political economists on the question of the causes for the rise of rents relying on an ingenious deduction (Whewell 1862, 72). Whewell recommended the replacement of the deductive method of reasoning "that of Ricardo and his school" with induction. "Their method," he argued, "consists in taking definitions, and reasoning downwards from them, as is done in geometry . . . In the other method we begin not from definitions, but from facts . . . And this method is the more useful, because the truths to which we are thus led are those which are characteristic of the social and political condition of each people; of the relations of rank; and of the means and chances of change and progress" (Whewell 1862, 84).

What is the relevance of this discussion to the consideration of Section F of the BAAS? Morrell and Thackray report that Whewell, as President-elect for the 1841 meeting, regarded with alarm the provocative nature of the discussions of Section F. His worry was twofold: on the one hand he thought that these sorts of discussions ran against the espoused principles and outlook of the BAAS, and as such might undermine the reputation sought for it by the gentlemen of science; and on the other hand he worried that the political positions openly taken during these discussions would undermine the ability of the BAAS to play its own political role as an effective—unified—lobby group (Morrell and Thackray 1981, 295).

Harvey William Becher provides a broader explanation of Whewell's objection to Section F. According to Becher, "Whewell had definite views on the legitimate bounds of science, but religion was not one of them." In 1841 Whewell threatened to resign from the BAAS if the members of the Statistics Section, including "both eminent and notorious men" such as Thomas Chalmers and Robert Owen continued to gather data for a new Poor Law and to discuss the "most inflammatory and agitating questions of the day." Denouncing the statisticians in his Presidential Address to the BAAS, Whewell reminded his audience that they lacked the conviction of their predecessors in the other sciences who freely exalted their topic in science while embracing religion. As Becher concludes, "For Whewell, scientific analysis of social welfare exceeded the bounds of legitimate science; religion was the inevitable end of science" (Becher 1971, 134).

It is quite true that religious considerations had something to do with Whewell's outrage, but to limit his objection to Section F only to these would be a grave oversimplification. In addition to "purely scientific issues," issues related to the "appropriate" methodology of science and the subject-matter which it should study, there seemed to have been other concerns that also agitated Whewell. According to O. J. R. Howarth, himself a secretary of the BAAS in the 1930s, Section F was originally to consist of statistics alone, and Whewell's anger stemmed from the fact that Section F was involved in the discussion of the Poor Laws, which were the focus of much social and political debate. Whewell argued that "it was impossible to listen to the proceedings of the Statistical section without perceiving that they involved exactly what it was most necessary and most desired to exclude from the proceedings." He continued to wonder "who would propose . . . an ambulatory body, composed partly of men of reputation and partly of a miscellaneous crowd, to go round year by year from town to town and at each place discuss the most inflammatory and agitating questions of the day?" (Howarth 1931, 87).

It seems that it was acceptable, in Whewell's view, to disagree and argue about scientific methods of inquiry, including political economy; but it was quite contrary to anything he believed in to disagree and argue about social and political matters in a "scientific manner" within "scientific associations." The proper place for such discussions was the political institutions of London. In this sense, then, Whewell maintained the ideology of science—a peaceful, value-neutral, and objective pursuit based on empirical data that is clearly demarcated from the social and political discourse—as it was interpreted by the gentlemen of science, the leaders of the BAAS.

Put in these terms, it would seem that Whewell would denounce any attempt to bring political considerations into the scientific discourse, because considerations of this sort would taint the "purity" of science. But, as became obvious from Whewell's arguments, Whewell recognized the "political" nature of the organization and its potential for upholding the status quo or for reform. Since he represented the dominance of the conservative attitudes of the Anglican academics who influenced the proceedings of the BAAS, Whewell did not wish the BAAS to turn into a reform movement that threatened the political establishment in London. Politicizing the scientific discourse consciously for lobbying efforts in one particular direction was one thing, but opening the scientific discourse to a multiplicity of radical proposals from around the Empire was quite another and unacceptable thing.

The early years of the controversy surrounding the proceedings of Section F only foreshadow the major crisis that evolved during the late 1870s, culminating in a concerted effort to "abolish" Section F from the BAAS altogether. Imagine, for a moment, what this action symbolizes. To expel a student from school is not unusual, as long as the action is explained, follows certain guidelines, and is publicly acknowledged. To expel a club member because of unacceptable behavior or violation of club rules is unusual but not exceptional. But to expel an entire section or field of research or discipline from an organization is quite rare. One may sanction a group, country, or discipline, as is often done in the United Nations; one may even suspend one's membership because of overdue bills or nonpayment of membership fees. There was no effort to reconstitute Section F or move its constituent disciplines —political economy and statistics—into other sections of the BAAS. As such, the episode surrounding the unsuccessful attempt to expel Section F from the BAAS is unique.

Just as the debates about the "legitimacy" of Section F of the early years of the BAAS had a prestigious spokesman, Whewell, so the debates in the 1870s had an equally prominent spokesman, Francis Galton. It seems worth considering, even if only briefly, the specific background of the second assault on Section F, just as the specific background of the early years of the BAAS helps explain why people like Whewell worried about the disrepute into which the association might sink once the controversial subject-matters of Section F became public.

Gerard M. Koot asserts that by the 1870s orthodox political economy was in full crisis, a crisis that was simultaneously internal and external (Koot 1980, 178). Koot echoes the sentiment suggested by Coats that during that period English political economy suffered a considerable loss of public prestige (Coats 1954, 143). The "crisis" and "loss of public prestige" culminated in what has become known as the English or British "*Methodenstreit*," drawing its name and its discursive framework from its German counterpart, but having distinct British characteristics (Koot 1980, 196).

Koot explains what was the major contribution of the British historical school, and what it hoped to achieve. Recalling the works of Arnold Toynbee, William James Ashley, and H. S. Foxwell, Koot claims that British historical economics reached its fullest development when attempting to construct a distinctly historical economics. These economists in particular can be perceived as social reformers, even as "English socialists," who hoped to employ economic history and applied economics as a means by which "to mold a more orderly capitalist society" (Koot 1980, 186). The complexity of the issues undertaken by the British *Methodenstreit* concerning the methodology of economics, cannot be reduced to those of its German counterpart. There were political matters to be considered, too; and personalities played an important role in the conflict. But even if one focuses exclusively on the methodological aspect of the debate, one would find that the insistence on the employment of historically relevant material was a move toward some form of adding and integrating induction (as opposed to the exclusive employment of deduction) so that economic policies would be perceived as hypotheses open to empirical testing, that is, confirmation or refutation.[11]

It is interesting to note that the general hostility to political economy was not confined to the BAAS, as Coats reports. According to Coats, one of the "crudest" attacks (that might have inspired the proposal to expel Section F) was made by Bonamy Price, a professor of political economy at Oxford. Price contended that the current "wild passion for scientific treatment" was indeed unwarranted, since political economy was not a science but a practical study. "What are called economic laws by most writers are merely tendencies. As such, they cannot profess absolute and uniform character. Political economy is therefore nothing more nor less than the application of common sense to familiar processes" (Coats 1954, 145). Given Price's contentions of the time, it seems that the BAAS episode can be viewed as symptomatic of the politicization of academic research in the history of political economy. In a similar fashion, the episode discussed here is symptomatic of certain attitudes toward science and certain expectations of scientists as experts not to be involved in political disputes.

V: THE ATTACK BY GALTON

The official reports of the BAAS for the 1870s (which are promptly published a year after a meeting takes place) are not as helpful as one would hope for reconstructing the attack on Section F. There is no official presidential address of either the BAAS or of any section in which the attack against Section F is explicitly mentioned. William Spottiswoode, as president of the BAAS in 1878, refers only casually to the limits which must be put on those wishing to participate and present papers at the BAAS meetings. His address steers clear from mentioning Section F, but those who knew what resolutions were adopted a year earlier in the Council Committee could discern his own approval from his vague remarks about the importance of presenting material which is considered scientific, that is, material based on empirical evidence.

If presidential addresses are indicators of the general atmosphere and attitude of their association, then Thomas Andrews in 1876 led his audience to believe that all was well with Section F. His remarks included a statement about the important growth of "three new sciences" in the past century: experimental chemistry, political economy, and mechanical engineering (BAASR 1877, lxviii–lxix). During that meeting, Sir George Campbell addressed Section F and explained the historical and philosophical connection between statistics and economics. If anything, one could have had the impression that economics was coming closer to being considered "economic science," as Campbell called it.

But the Report of 1877 contains the clues to what took place—behind the curtains, so to speak—at the BAAS in connection with the status of Section F. Though Professor Allen Thomson's presidential address surprisingly had no intimation of what had taken place during the deliberations of the General Committee that year in Plymouth, the Report of the Council, which was presented to the General

Committee, includes the following:

> The attention of the Council having been drawn to the character of some of the Sectional Proceedings at late Meetings of the Association, a Committee was appointed to consider and report to the Council on the possibility of excluding unscientific or otherwise unsuitable papers and discussions from the Sectional Proceedings of the association.
>
> The Committee recommended that papers which have been reported on unfavourably by the Organizing Committee shall not be brought before the Sectional Committees, and that, in the rules for conducting the business of the Sectional Committees, the following rules should be inserted, viz.:—
>
> 1. The President shall call on the Secretary to read the minutes of the previous Meeting of the Committee.
>
> 2. No paper shall be read until it has been formally accepted by the Committee of the Section, and entered on the minutes accordingly.
>
> The Council proposes that this alteration of rules shall be carried into effect.
>
> The Committee in their Report further considered that some of the subjects brought before Section F could not be considered scientific in the ordinary sense of that word, and that the question of the discontinuance of Section F deserved the serious consideration of the Council.
>
> The Council have requested the Committee to report more fully the reasons which had induced them to come to this conclusion, but the Committee have not yet made a further report. (BAASR 1878, xlix)

To begin with, these recommendations, especially those numbered 1 and 2 were adopted that year, and remain part of the Rules of the Association to this day. Reading the report carefully, one can observe the generality with which the problem of "unscientific" presentations was addressed at first, and the specific attack on Section F that followed. Why was Section F singled out? It is clear from some of the opening remarks of sectional presidents of these years that other sciences were also trying to improve their scientific credibility and show the rest of the BAAS that indeed they belong in that prestigious community (e.g., anatomy, physiology, and geography). Why was the attack focused on those "subjects" that "could not be considered scientific in the ordinary sense of that word," rather than on the Section as a whole? Was this a strategic move to ensure the "serious consideration" of "the question of the discontinuance of Section F" or a move that would not dismiss all papers in this section categorically but most of them, one by one?

Reading this report, one has no clear idea who the critics were, and what criteria of "science" they were using. What was "the ordinary sense of the word" science? Though we recall the ideology of science ascribed to in the early years of the BAAS, there seem to have been additional concerns during the 1870s. The pivotal role of Francis Galton becomes evident when finding the pamphlet he distributed to the committee appointed by the Council to examine Section F. The pamphlet is in the BAAS archives, and its content became public when published (with an editorial note of disapproval and the response to it) in the *Journal of the Statistical Society* in 1877.[12]

Galton, in a methodic and "inductive" fashion, listed 71 titles of papers that have been read before Section F, and then concluded that "not a single memoir treats of the mathematical theory of Statistics," and if any were to fit that category it would undoubtedly be properly presented in Section A (Mathematics). Galton conceded that Section F "deals with numerous and important matters of human knowledge." But, he quickly added, "this is not of itself a title to the existence of the Section", because other equally important areas of research, such as history, "are by common consent inappropriate subjects for the British Association." In general, Galton claimed that Section F incorporated such subjects that have in effect departed "so widely from the scientific ideal as to make them unsuitable for the British Association" (Galton 1877, 2–3).

Besides arguing that Section F is obsolete—if the subject is indeed "scientific" then it belongs in other sections and if it is not then it does not belong anywhere in the BAAS—Galton made the following charge. "Also that as the Section is isolated and avowedly attracts much more than its share of persons of both sexes who have had no scientific training, its discussions are apt to become even less scientific than they would otherwise have been." This charge was especially troublesome to Galton because of his concern that any "discredit" engendered by one section will be borne by the BAAS as a whole. And finally, Galton also argued that the less sections the easier the management of the BAAS, and the less problems will affect the successful arrangements for annual meetings (Galton 1877, 4). Galton concluded his attack by suggesting that Section F find a more "congenial" home in the Social Science Congress where presumably less scientific or a different scientific rigor was required. Galton's specific wording and arguments can be clearly detected in the Report of the BAAS quoted above, even though he is never mentioned by name.

With the exception of the report in one statistical journal (as part of the section titled "Miscellanea" at the end of the 1877 issue), no direct association with Galton is attributed in the official reports of the BAAS. Moreover, Galton himself does not mention this episode (though devoting a chapter to the BAAS) in his autobiography. Committed as he was to the ideals of the BAAS, Galton curiously spends more pages in his autobiography on his parentage and twice as many pages to discuss his experiences at Cambridge than on this central episode (Galton 1908). Howarth is one of the few who reports Galton's attack and quotes parts thereof (Howarth 1931, 89).

"Running" the BAAS was the exclusive undertaking of a few individuals, all of whom "deserved" the title of gentlemen of science, none of whom would ever be personally involved in anything as scandalous as the presentation of inflammatory material or controversial intellectual findings. Though the BAAS was conceived as a different institution than the Royal Society—less "stuffy" and "clubbish," more open to the concerns of the public—it nevertheless did not fully avoid the pretense and self-proclaimed importance that comes with the territory. The leadership of the BAAS can be viewed, as many commentators do, from a laudatory perspective, with the respect due to great minds at work; but it can also be viewed as a group of individuals whose autocratic behavior and personal intrigues played a significant role in the establishment and promotion of "scientific" activity at the time. They had the control not merely to monitor the activities of their peers, but also to dictate the directions they took.

One notable example of the stature of a leader in the BAAS, and an example relevant to the case of Section F is Galton. Galton's scientific standing and his various roles within the British scientific community are also directly relevant to the position he took against Section F. A close review of his own background, personal and intellectual, and his own judgments concerning statistics and economics (mostly reported by others, and hardly mentioned in his own writings), are of interest here. Such a review will further an appreciation to what extent there is any justification for an attack on economics by other scientists, or for that matter on any other discipline. (For example, Galton's development of "national" eugenics as an alleged scientific endeavor has been perceived to be racist and unscientific, that is, falling outside the confines of the "pure" scientific method as delineated in the BAAS.)[13] For instance, who is setting the standards for the evaluation of any field of inquiry? Are personal prestige and connections, as Galton had, enough to shield one from the criticism of the scientific community? Is having been granted membership in the scientific community sufficient grounds for dismissing any future challenges? Some provisional answers to these questions may be conjectured by reviewing Galton's role in attempting to banish Section F from the BAAS. To be sure, Galton is used here to exemplify the sort of behavior endemic to scientists in leadership roles and not in order to fully examine his life and works.

Galton's devoted biographer and disciple, Karl Pearson, explains at length Galton's involvement in the BAAS, and the specific role he played in pressing the abolishment of Section F. Pearson reports that the Council of the BAAS had been "much troubled" by the proceedings of that section and appointed a committee to report on the possibility of excluding that section from the BAAS. Pearson says that "while Galton reserved a final judgment the remarks he put before the committee were adverse to the maintenance of Section F." This way of setting the record on the incident, of course, minimizes the force of Galton's statements, given Galton's pamphlet and Pearson's quote of parts thereof (Pearson 1924, 347–348). Pearson portrays Galton's behavior in this way so as to illustrate that Galton did not have a "slavish admiration of all types of statistics" (Pearson 1924, 347). Though it is true that Galton did not unequivocally argue that Section F fails to fulfill the "criteria of science" at the time, his comments lend themselves to a great deal of doubt that one should vote in favor of retaining Section F in the organization. As already noted above, Galton's argument undermines any potential response, for it says that if Section F contains statistically significant papers, then it should be incorporated into Section A (thus eliminating Section F as such); and if not, then it should be abolished altogether.

Pearson interprets these remarks generously and claims that Galton's attack was not aimed at Section F per se, but rather at the way in which statistics was practiced at the time. Galton's attack, according to Pearson, could have likewise been leveled against the Royal Statistical Society itself. So, what was Galton's aim? Pearson claims that according to Galton "probably the right procedure would have been to permeate Section F with the newer type of statisticians" (Pearson 1924, 348). This might have been the case, that is, a call for reform and change in the practices of a group of "scientists," no matter what exactly is meant by the "newer type of statisticians"; but this interpretation does not coincide with Galton's own words (as quoted above) that he could not find any such thing as mathematical statistics. Besides, must a call for reform and change be couched in a threat for expulsion? Was Galton the rigid "mathematical physicist" Pearson calls him, or was he an innovative statistician of a future generation? A partial answer may be obtained from Galton's remarks on his view of science.

According to Galton: "Until the phenomena of any branch of knowledge have been submitted to measurement and number it cannot assume the dignity of a science" (Pearson 1922, 10). A similar notion is echoed in Galton's assertion that you should "count when-ever you can" (Pearson 1924, 347). Was Galton after all a "slave" to anything mathematical, and not, as Pearson claims, someone who had no "slavish admiration of all types of statistics?" Discounting Galton's own proclamations, Pearson asserts that Galton was a great scientist whose outlook was wider than that of his cousin Charles Darwin. Galton was a social reformer as well, appealing to "knowledge" and not mere sentiment.[14] Presumably, Galton used statistics only as a tool of his craft, and was not obsessed with the fruits of that tool. No, concludes Pearson, Galton was not mentally enslaved to the power of statistics, numbers, and quantification. If not mentally enslaved, was he then using "measurements" and statistics as scientific mortar to enforce his personal views? More pertinent to the case of Section F, one can ask: If Galton was indeed open-minded, why was he so concerned with the content of the papers delivered in a section that was not even his own?

Galton's own scientific reputation was impeccable: his genealog-ical pedigree was one of the finest in the scientific community (shar-ing with Charles Darwin the same maternal grandfather) and his institutional affiliations in Britain commanded respect. Given this reputation, there was a wide perception that he had the authority to adjudicate any scientific matter, even one outside his immediate area of specialization. From all the references we have of Galton's view of science, scientific method, and the "proper" discourse of science, it seems that Galton probably favored a restricted and hence "pro-fessionalized" scientific discourse, that is, a discourse that in its claims for ideological purity overlooks its own ideological pre-suppositions. And this preference, especially as it pertains to the specialization of scientific research, according to John Maloney, may explain his hostility to Section F (Maloney 1985, 3–21).

Galton's crusade against Section F in a fashion different from Whewell's cannot be evaluated exclusively according to the pre-sumed criteria of demarcation used to qualify a field of inquiry as sci-entific. As mentioned earlier, the political atmosphere and pressure surrounding the works of scientists was not limited to economists dealing with strikes or the Poor Laws. Amidst a period of prosper-ity, when the sun never set on the British Empire and when colonial expansion led the British to encounter other people primarily as objects of consumption (from raw materials to slavery), political con-victions and class affiliation played an important role (recall Morrell and Thackray's deliberate designation "gentlemen" to describe the sci-entists of the BAAS) in forming the views of scientists.

More specifically, one can appreciate the political hues that colored scientific debates in the case of Darwin's impact on the scientific community (as is noted below concerning Ingram's Address in response to the attack by Galton). The scientific establishment was immensely influenced by Darwin's principles and theory of evolution (after the publication in 1859 of *The Origin of Species*), not least of whom, his relative Galton. Darwin's pronouncements not only challenged divine intervention in the process of creation, but also laid out the foundation for any understanding of human development and the interaction among individuals in a society. The "social Darwinists" used Darwin's scientific claims to bolster their ideological commitment to a conservative political order (maintenance of the status quo) and the continuation of a class-structure, arguing, in the process, that traits were hereditary. Galton's eugenics (already mentioned in 1869 but formally coined in 1883) is a deliberate attempt to quantify (and thereby legitimate scientifically) a study of human features and behavior in hereditary terms so as to distinguish among individuals and races and explain their inherent differences, differences that remain insurmountable no matter what social programs one introduces to overcome them (e.g., Hofstadter 1955, 161–167). It seems that Galton was more partisan than Whewell in his attack on the seemingly radical Section F, invoking indirectly his own conservative convictions and trying to support them scientifically. Oddly enough, just as Section F members used "their science" to resolve a strike, so did Galton use "his science" to prop his political views.

Before turning to the responses (Farr's and Ingram's) that followed this last attack of 1877, it is worth noting some similarities (and a continuity of sorts) between Whewell's and Galton's criticisms of Section F. First, they both questioned the credentials of those involved with the section. While Whewell questioned the reputation of some of those involved with the section in general terms, Galton was explicit in his disapproval of the participation of women (according to Howarth's record). So, while Whewell's concern about "credentials"—of participants and audience—can be understood in light of his wish to acquire the prestige his association deserved, Galton's concern seems more clearly sexist.[15]

It was both unfair and unreasonable to charge that economists were in any respect unique in their lack of "proper" credentials. It was common in those days, as we can tell from the degrees listed after the names of the participants, that the credentials of "scientists" varied from person to person. Unlike present day meetings in which most participants hold a doctorate in their respective fields, in those days lawyers were involved in geographical studies, and members of the clergy discussed organic chemistry. So, the issue of credentials, without a specified criteria acceptable by all bona fide scientists, seems irrelevant. (Incidentally, the same was true not only in Britain but also in the United States.)

As for the issue of credentials in gender terms, that is, that women by definition could not have the proper credentials, this now becomes an issue of sexism. Whether or not it is sexist can be ascertained partially from the scant data available on women's participation in the BAAS. Noting that the BAAS admitted "members of both sexes" quite in advance of other scientific bodies, and that the number of women has ranged from 600 to 1058, Dr. William Farr, in his response to Galton's attack, pointed out that since its inception Section F has had 21 papers read by women. Among the more notable women who participated in the section, Farr named Florence Nightingale (Pamphlet, 6). (This is a far better record than that of the AAAS; see also note 15.)

In spite of this relatively positive record, one that could be used to argue that the BAAS was not a sexist organization, it should be noted that the Report of the Council of the BAAS of 1875–1876 records the following resolution: "That it does not appear to have been the practice of the British Association to elect Ladies as officers of the Association, or to place them upon the General or Sectional Committees; and they are of opinion that no case has been made out for altering the practice hitherto in force." (Archives of the BAAS, Bodleian Library, Oxford). Once again, the leadership of the BAAS (the gentle*men* of science), was not enthusiastic about the participation of women in section meetings and especially wanted to guard the leadership from an infiltration of women who might "take it over" and "lower" the scientific standards of the Association. So, though women were not discouraged from participating (even noting the "half price" incentive for membership fees), the BAAS leadership was not about to consider women scientists their intellectual and social equals (or capable of leading a scientific association). Herein, then, lies the sexism of enlightened and scientifically admired leaders, such as Whewell and Galton: when it gets to sharing power or changing power relations, women are feared and therefore discriminated against.

Second, Whewell and Galton were concerned in a similar manner about the content of the papers presented in Section F. Were members of Section F studying "pure science" or were they concerned with practical matters, involved in "applied science"? Farr (in his report of the Committee investigating the possibility of discontinuing Section F) and Howarth much later recall the 1874 strike in the linen mills of Belfast which coincided with the annual meeting of the BAAS at that city. Since in Section F matters of union organization and strikes were discussed, its meeting turned into the mediation ground for the strikers and owners of the mills. The meetings of this section helped resolve the conflict and end the strike. Was this an example for the inapplicability of economics? Or was this an example of how applied economic research works and therefore how impure it is in terms of its scientific credentials?

Recalling the standards and criteria of science that guided the leadership of the BAAS, especially in terms of the hierarchy of the sciences and the demarcation between pure and applied science, one can appreciate the concerns Whewell and Galton had. But, one may ask: at what costs were they willing to launch attacks on Section F? What would be the consequences of challenging an entire field of inquiry? How would such a challenge affect other disciplines?

VI: THE DEFENSE BY INGRAM

It should be mentioned that before Ingram's defense there was one other attempt at blocking Galton's attack (mentioned briefly above). Attached to the pamphlet Galton circulated among the members of the BAAS Council was William Farr's response. His response included a letter sent by the secretaries of the Statistical Society and other relevant materials that could be used as part of the considerations "favourable to the maintenance of Section F." Three issues are raised in this response.

First, the notion of "scientific" propriety is extended to all other sections, so that poor judgments in the acceptance of papers is not limited to Section F. Second, the complaint about large attendance is transformed into an argument about the great contribution of the section in drawing new (dues paying) members. Besides, this issue is especially significant in light of the fact that Section F has received only a very small portion of grants over the years. So, one could argue, the difference between revenue and expenses was benefiting the BAAS as a whole. Third, questions about the credentials of the leaders of Section F (namely, that none was ever asked to be the President of the BAAS) can be laid to rest when considering such formidable members as John Mills (who contributed to business cycle analysis and was president and an active member of the Manchester Statistical Society) who would not have embarrassed the BAAS (Pamphlet, 5–8). Farr's report indicates that Galton's attack can either be launched at all the sections (including F) of the BAAS or it must be withdrawn. One may wonder what specifically drew these two leaders of the statistical community to part company on this matter. Was there a personal rivalry between Galton and Farr that found an outlet in this incident?

Here is a conjecture. Galton was a council member of the Statistical Society during 1877–78, when Farr was an honorary vice-president, and while Farr was vice president of the Royal Society, Galton was a Fellow of that Society. These "offices" may indicate some rivalry or competition. Another interesting place to find some personal friction is in the ledger records concerning grants received from the BAAS. The only recipients of grants in the anthropometric committee were Dr. Beddoe £100, Dr. Farr £200, and Mr. F. Galton £80 (BAAS archives, 1871–1882 ledger, 201, Bodleian Library, Oxford). Was Galton resentful that Farr received more money than he?

J. K. Ingram's presidential address of Section F in 1878 has become a landmark statement of the changing nature and methods of study of economists during the 1870s in Britain. Apparently it had made some impression outside the BAAS as well. Coats reports that Ingram's address met with an enthusiastic response in America and in Germany. Being influenced by Comte, Ingram emphasized the need for a unified science of society. According to Coats, the parallel between sociology and biology was central in the Address, and the "organic analogy" loomed large in the exposition (Coats 1954, 146–147; Maloney 1985, 18–19). Ingram's address opens with the following statements:

> An important crisis in the history of our Section has taken place. Its claim to form a part of the British Association has been disputed. Some of the cultivators of the older branches of research but half recognize the right of Political Economy and Statistics to citizenship in the commonwealth of science; and it is not obscurely intimated on their part that these studies would do well to relinquish pretensions which cannot be sustained, and proceed, with or without shame, to take the lower room to which alone they are entitled. (BAASR 1878, 641).

Upon reading these few lines one can immediately appreciate how seriously the threat of expulsion was taken by the leading economists of the day. Talking about a "crisis" and about the "right" of "citizenship in the commonwealth of science," Ingram instilled in his audience a great sense of urgency. The words he chose seem not only to express his own anxiety or anger but also to have been used in the manifesto of the critics. It is they who charged that economics had no "right" of "citizenship," and it is they who charged economics with "pretensions"; and it is they, presumably, who mentioned terms like "shame" and "the lower room" to which economists belonged, as they were recorded in the official records of the BAAS.

Most critics did not openly object to the subject matter chosen by economists for their inquiries, as was previously noted in the cases of Whewell and Galton, but focused instead on the methods employed by economists. A discussion of and a decision about methodology, economists themselves agreed, if deemed acceptable by other scientists, will necessarily legitimize the choices economists have made about what subjects to study. For any subject may be studied (this freedom is cherished by all), so long as it is studied scientifically. But what if the subject one wishes to study cannot be approached scientifically, or if approached scientifically requires a different set of methods? It seems that since Adam Smith economists have accepted on faith their putative ability to examine economic matters in a scientific fashion similar (if not identical) to other sciences.

With this in mind, it is possible to examine the specific arguments and linguistic approach Ingram used to defend economics against its critics. His address remains an important exemplar in the defense of the scientific status of economics, since the use it made of biological terms inspired future generations of economists, as well as maintained some of the prejudices (in favor of certain analogies between economics and biology) already present in Smith's work. For example, Foley argues for the hypothesis that "important elements of Adam Smith's thought were consciously, systematically, and secretly modeled after a system of physical, biological, and social evolution which he found in the ancients" (Foley 1976, xi, 55), and that Smith's thought is intimately connected to Descartes' and Harvey's theories on blood circulation as the foundation of liquid circulation apparent in Quesnay's *Tableau Economique* of 1758 (Foley 1976, Ch. 7: "The Physician Economist", 120–138).

Though Ingram acknowledged at the end of his address that "it is impossible to vindicate for Statistics the character of a science," and though he proposed that "the field of the Section should be enlarged, so as to comprehend the whole of Sociology," he still maintained that the expulsion of economics from the BAAS "would be a degradation of the Association" (BAASR 1878, 656–657). He argued that economics must remain part of the BAAS, for it contained important elements of the "study of mankind." The argument that runs throughout his address is embedded in biological terms, and draws extensively from the actual study of biology.

Ingram quoted from Huxley that "The study of living bodies is really one discipline, which is divided into zoology and botany simply as a matter of convenience" (BAASR 1878, 645). The fact that zoology and botany are separated for the purpose of research does not mean that the one is "more scientific" or "preferable" in any sense than the other, or that they compete with each other for scientific status so that if one receives it the other cannot. On the contrary, the argument goes, they both draw from the "undisputed" importance and validity of biology as a subject worthy of intellectual efforts and scientific considerations. As such, these fields of inquiry are branches of biology, and as branches gain their strength from the strong roots and trunk of biology.

Why did Ingram propose an analogy with biology? He tried to argue that economics should be also understood as a branch of the social sciences, and as such could draw its importance and validity from the "undisputed fact" that the study of humankind includes also the study of economic factors and conditions. Anthropology, for example, was accepted at the BAAS as a science—especially since Galton was identified then as an anthropologist—and if it deserved that coveted scientific status and was itself considered a "branch" of the social sciences, then economics should be able to fare as well as anthropology.

Ingram continued his use of analogies from biology in order to promote the idea that when one examines the "living whole," one thereby undertakes to study the various interactions between its elements, rather than study the various aspects of the living whole separately. In the same manner, argued Ingram, if one is to study society "which is in so many respects kindred to biology," then one is required to study "the material well-being of society, its industrial constitution and development." (BAASR 1878, 646)

Ingram concluded this line of argument by explaining that the "human evolution" which humankind underwent is an important phenomenon worthy of scientific study. (Pearson's comparison between Darwin and Galton on this issue is relevant here. Darwin's immense influence at the time forced most thinkers to mention somehow or actually employ Darwin's terminology, even though they were not concerned with the full implications of his theory.) The study of human evolution must consist of economic factors and data pertinent to that evolution. As such, the dynamic part of the study of sociology can benefit from the scientific treatment of economic circumstances. As an example, Ingram cited the work of Adam Smith, whose scholarly eminence was undisputed among any audience at the BAAS.

Ingram's extensive employment of biological images and terminology was similar to those deployed by other economists during the end of the nineteenth century and therefore his address can be viewed as a representation of the prevailing attitude and intellectual orientation toward questions of scientific validity. Economists at this period thought it obvious and useful to employ biological analogies in an attempt to understand social processes, a general feeling or change of perspective that was justified from their perspective in light of the great influence in scientific circles of the ideas of Spencer and Darwin.

An attempt to reconstruct the tale of Section F would remain incomplete if no mention is made of Alfred Marshall whose ideas and works came to dominate economic theory well into the twentieth century. Marshall himself argued in his essay "Mechanical and Biological Analogies in Economics" that "it has been well said that analogies may help one into the saddle, but are encumbrances on a long journey. It is well to know when to introduce them, it is even better to know when to stop them off" (Marshall 1898, 314). But he still believed that "the Mecca of the economist is economic biology rather than economic dynamics" (Marshall 1898, 318).

Marshall only exemplifies the traditional use of biology traced back to Adam Smith and continued with Ingram, but as an important leader of political economy and a spokesman for its methodological commitments, his works include references to biology in a manner even more pronounced than in Ingram's address. Laurence Moss notes Marshall's reference to Darwin in his *Principles*, and Marshall's insistence on accepting the Lyell-Darwin view of slow, continuous, and incremental natural changes (Moss 1982, 3–4). J. Hirshleifer tried to trace some of the implications of Marshall's view that "economics is a branch of biology. Or, in more sweeping terms, of the contention that the social sciences generally can fruitfully be regarded as the sociobiology of the human species" (Hirshleifer 1977, 51). He then states his general and main thesis, a thesis that has become a standard for those studying "Economics from a Biological Viewpoint." "*The fundamental organizing concept of the dominant analytical structures employed in economics and in sociobiology are strikingly parallel.*" This means that "concepts" such as scarcity, competition, and equilibrium play similar roles in both biology and economics, and that "terminological pairs" such as species/industry, mutation/innovation, and evolution/progress, "have more or less analogous denotations" (Hirshleifer 1977, 1–2). A. L. Levine, for example, quotes from appendix C of Marshall's *Principles*: "Economics has no near kinship with any physical science. It is a branch of biology broadly interpreted" (Levine 1983, 277). According to Levine's summary, Marshall's "economy-in-a-biosystem" conception goes deeper than an analogy (Levine 1983, 284).

From the "original" sources available from the period, from "secondary" sources that comment on the works cited here, one begins to see a picture that is slowly drawn by the leadership of political economy, a picture whose contours become more clearly distinguishable as the years go by. But was this a unique occurrence at the time? From the records of the BAAS it is impossible to detect a similar incident, a similar effort to expel a discipline and a counter-effort to preserve the "scientific integrity" of a discipline. In this respect, then, the story of Section F is highly informative: it was no mere self-doubt that brought about a self-reflection and a reevaluation of a discipline's convictions and commitments; instead, external pressure forced an immediate introspection resulting in a proclamation, a declaration of purpose.

The declaration of political economy could have been the declaration of numerous other disciplines or sections of the BAAS. Perhaps it was a historical contingency that brought political economy to the attention of others; perhaps it was its "fate"; or perhaps it was a coincidence that certain personalities clashed during a particular time. Be that as it may, Ingram's address was not merely aimed to draw a linguistic parallel between the discourses of biology and political economy. One strategy he used to persuade his audience that economics is worthy of its membership in the BAAS was the inclusion of a set of "concrete" suggestions that economists and presumably statisticians should follow. Since the suggestions were perceived by him as methodological in nature—reflecting the standards of science prevalent in the BAAS—he expected them not to be dismissed as mere linguistic compromises but as fundamental commitments. In some respects, these suggestions provide an outline or even a manifesto of sorts that codified what Ingram and the leadership of political economy in Britain at the time took to be the most important and fundamental building blocks of their theoretical research.

The first suggestion stipulated that "the study of the economic phenomena of society ought to be systematically combined with that of the other aspects of social existence." On the whole this suggestion was not heeded, for in the desire to turn economics into a bona fide science, the emphasis has been on quantification rather than integration with other areas of the social sciences (See Jevons 1871 and Sassower 1985).

The second suggestion was that "the excessive tendency to abstraction and to unreal simplification should be checked." In many ways we can observe that on this account, too, the field has failed to follow Ingram's advice. There are still criticisms concerning the "unreal" elements—in terms of assumptions and definitions—with which economic theories and models are constructed. Ingram's suggestion that the complexity of the field be acknowledged and preserved is lost even within the advanced work of econometrics. As Marshall said some years after Ingram's address, when discussing "The Present Position of Economics": "The shift from the mathematico-physical sciences to the biological sciences has swept into economics, and thus there is a realization that economic conditions as well as the conditions of people must be appreciated developmentally, evolutionary, progressively." (Marshall 1885, 154–155).

The third suggestion was that "the a priori deductive method should be changed for the historical." This was the most important methodological concession, and one which could immediately qualify economic research as "scientific." It should be noted that the "historical" method is understood by Ingram to mean the empirical method that is informed by historical phenomena (i.e., induction) and, for example, not historical in Hegelian terms. This shows the impact of the British *Methodenstreit* and the inroads the British historical school was making. (Coats 1954, Koot 1980, and Maloney 1985). On this account, too, the suggestion was not followed, for the continued aspiration to new intellectual and technological heights through generalization and abstraction is evident in the push to set "models" for how a certain state of affairs is affected or will affect other conditions in the economy.

The fourth and last suggestion was that "economic laws and the practical prescriptions founded on those laws should be conceived and expressed in a less absolute form." This last recommendation is in some sense the most problematic, for it encourages the sort of vagueness (or relativism) against which Ingram himself warned in his second suggestion. Moreover, Ingram's formulation gives room for the potential misuse of economic laws. If economic laws are stated in a "less absolute form" because of the complexity of the data they attempt to cover and explain, then they may give rise to "prescriptions" that are even less precise and thus open for manipulations by those proposing or executing them. And finally, once economic conditions or situations are not formulated as "laws," whether "absolute" or not (must a law by definition be absolute?), how can they be perceived as "scientific" in the sense advocated during that time?

VII: CONCLUSION

Ingram's argument that the likeness of zoology and botany is mirrored in the studies of economics was meant as an illustration through which he hoped economics could ascend to the scientific level of these two other branches of biology. He took for granted that biology, and all its associated branches, were bona fide sciences deserving their status. But were they? Except for some of Farr's comments concerning the possibility that economics was not the only science that would not stand up under Galton's criteria for scientific legitimacy (however construed), it seems that Ingram himself and others close to him did not turn the tables on the other sciences in order to challenge their right to belong to the scientific establishment as well. Ingram's success, as stated above, can be understood in terms of his ability to convince skeptics that economics deserves to remain in the BAAS. On the other hand, Ingram's failure can be understood in terms of his inability to probe into the very nature of scientific inquiry in an attempt to reevaluate scientific procedures and the criteria by which inquiries were judged to be scientific. Perhaps the time was not ripe for challenging the prominent and hegemonic position of "science" as such.

Retelling the story of the episode that took place at the BAAS lends itself to various interpretations. From the reconstruction of the episode one can learn to what extent professional activities are bound to remain autocratic and conservative, regardless of the proclaimed vision of the founders of professional institutions. That is, declarations of "principles" may serve the purpose of obfuscating critical scrutiny rather than be used as the parameters or limits within which activities are bound. In addition, once epistemological and methodological problems are identified in one discipline, do they reflect a more general state of affairs? Should one turn attacks like the one recalled here into an open debate in which any field, including physics, for example, will be under scrutiny for its fulfillment of specified scientific criteria, no matter how historically relative they may be? And finally, it is possible to read this episode as an illustration that "images" of science rather than "actual practices" dominate the attacks and defenses of the scientific status of fields of research. Images of science—what science should look like in the eyes of both practitioners and the public—are usually usurped from elsewhere, other fields, such as biology and physics, regardless of any discrepancies that may be detected between the image and the practice of those fields themselves.

Before moving to questions that arise from the present story and trying to answer them with a variety of additional stories, one may wonder how the present story "ended." Ingram's address, no matter how convincing or trivial, apparently had the effect its author anticipated. Today Section F still includes economics and the Section as a whole is still part of the BAAS. At least that much could be accomplished, even if the general public's suspicion of all matters economic may never be put to rest. Though Section F retained its membership, the story of the 1877 episode haunts it to the present. Historians know the story or at least parts thereof; they recall the outline of the story and make of it whatever they want for whatever purpose. Why is there continued interest and recollection? Perhaps the reason has to do with the ambiguity concerning what "science" is and is not, what it should aspire to be, and what its practitioners are committed to. While consenting to revamp the methodological apparatus by adopting the inductivism of the other sciences, Ingram still maintained that economic data were uniquely complex and as such were less susceptible to translation into scientific laws. This ambiguity is not exclusively in the domain of Section F. As will become clear in subsequent chapters, by the late twentieth century it is difficult to uphold a view of science that refers back to the standards proposed in the late nineteenth century or even before that period.

The present story includes not only a recollection of the records available in libraries and archives, but it also includes an atmosphere, a milieu, in which certain attitudes and aspirations become apparent. It was important for Section F not to be expelled, this much is obvious. But why? What specifically was at stake: prestige, status, financial rewards, social recognition? Whether one is a good member or a member in good standing seemed to bother Section F less than the threat of expulsion. Being thrown out of the BAAS would diminish the putative authority that could be claimed by members of Section F: their power in their own minds and in the mind of the public would evaporate. This situation is similar to the threat of being expelled from a church, being excommunicated, as Spinoza, for one, was.

The present narrative sets the stage for an examination of various problems facing our culture in terms of supporting a group of scientific experts in its midst, problems traceable but not limited to those mentioned in the present chapter. The chapters that follow use this narrative (in one way or another) as a point of departure; they are self-contained in one sense, yet mutually related in various other senses.

CHAPTER 2

On Oracles:
Psychological "Foundations" of Knowledge

I: INTRODUCTION

One of the lessons or legacies of the incident that occurred to Section F of the BAAS in the last century is that a group of scientists—some of the leaders of the BAAS—challenged another group of scientists—those involved in Section F. The challenge was not confined to the inner circles of the BAAS but became public knowledge. Can only scientists challenge other scientists, in the sense that their challenge is legitimized by their "scientific" credentials? Or, does the challenge by scientists open the door for others to challenge scientific judgments? The case of Section F seems to indicate that the reason for alarm by Section F was that Whewell and Galton were the challengers, as opposed to members of Parliament or members of the media. In fact, around that time, British courts of law agreed that the only legitimate doubt concerning scientific expert testimony could be advanced by other scientific expert testimony (more on that in chapter 3).

The enclosed community of scientists/experts of the British empire of the last century has not opened much; scientists legitimate or criticize one another, but the public's challenge can always be rebuffed by scientists as being hysteric or unwarranted. What are the historical precedents that have set up one group of individuals in a privileged position amidst their society and fellow citizens?

The story of Section F of the BAAS exemplifies a psycho-philosophical narrative that recurs in the history of ideas. Labeling the present narrative psycho-philosophical means in the present context the following. There was a time when questions were ultimately answered by oracles. "Oracles" had an unquestionable authority that allowed them to pronounce whatever messages from whatever "source" they deemed fit. But how were oracles installed, and who appealed to them? There are several answers to these questions, some dating to ancient Greece and some to sacred religious texts. Mentioning the oracles of Delphi and Shakespeare's reference to oracles, for example, will illustrate a duplicitous attitude towards oracles, expressing reverence to an "all-knowing" entity while suspecting all along that oracles know nothing at all.

Oracles' pronouncements in the form of predictions—as warnings or promises—are based on their "insight." Their insight is attributed either to divine revelation or to scientific investigation. In either case, there is an epistemological foundation that "justifies" the special status given to what oracles claim to know and what they say. Whether oracles are considered divine mouthpieces or are working scientists makes no difference in the public's eye in regards to their privileged (epistemological) position. I will argue here that any epistemological discourse is also psychological, so that psychological conditions and factors influence and are influenced by any epistemological claim (no matter how well or poorly grounded). And a psychological discourse raises questions of responsibility in ways different from those commonly raised by epistemological discourses.

We listen to oracles/scientists because it comforts us to listen to someone else who will tell us what we want to hear. When we admit to following the authoritative declaration of another, we in effect listen to what we ourselves would have said had we been given the opportunity to do so. It is possible to "follow ourselves" since the proliferation of scientists permits a greater variety of views and theories with a greater likelihood that an "appropriate" one will be found to fit one's own inclinations. The appeal to experts and specialists so common nowadays is a cultural appeal that is disguised in epistemological jargon but which is grounded in our psychological tendencies to find order in life and systematize, as much as possible, whatever information we gather (Sassower 1985, Ch. 3).

II: ORACLES

"Originally," the *Oxford English Dictionary* tells us, an oracle was "the instrumentality, agency, or medium, by which a god was supposed to speak or make known his will; the mouthpiece of the deity; the place or seat of such instrumentality, at which divine utterances were believed to be given." The notions of instrumentality and medium leave it ambiguous whether there is a physical object, a "thing" that is being referred to, or an individual, a person, or even a creature, who is the mouthpiece. An oracle can be both a place/location and a person who is in that place/location, and as long as a divine entity or a deity is "behind" the utterances, the oracle maintains its revered status. At the same time, it is not clear from these definitions whether the reference to an oracle is a reference to a person in a specified location or, more generally, "A response, decision, or message, given usually by a priest or priestess of a god, and, as was supposed, by his inspiration at the shrine or seat where the deity was supposed to be thus accessible to inquiries. These responses were for the most part obscure or ambiguous." The response or utterance, of course, is both a medium that transmits words or sentences from a "deity" to the people as well as a medium that uses another medium—a person—to deliver itself in a personified form.

Added to these ambiguities concerning the term "oracle" are other ambiguities that have found their way into contemporary uses of the term. These ambiguities anchor the prestige of the term or the awe with which it is treated commonly in a sense of divine mission that is at once authoritative and infallible. Being presumed infallible authorizes an oracle to an extent that is open to abuses, for no possible mistake can be attributed to it. For example, the *OED* refers to an oracle as "something regarded as an infallible guide or indicator, especially when its action is viewed as recondite or mysterious, as a chronometer, a compass." As a compass, an oracle guides its listeners toward a particular direction, it leads one to follow a path that is considered "appropriate" or even "best" in some sense. The thrust of this reference is forward, pointing to the future, assessing in advance the potential stored in one choice over another. But can an oracle always be trusted? Are oracles always "good" and have "good intentions" in their activities?

When the vision to the future is associated with a person who predicts, as opposed to a message or prediction detached from its originator, the *OED* says: "A person of great wisdom or knowledge, whose opinions or decisions are generally accepted; an authority reputed or affecting to be infallible." And with this reference, the audience, the recipients of the message or prediction, is alerted not only to the ability of an oracle to make a prediction, to tell someone what should be done but also to the credibility accompanying such utterances. The credibility of an oracle is not challenged, for one has to wait until the "prediction" is fulfilled or not in order to judge the prediction as true or false.

As such, an oracle, just like a Biblical prophecy, is "An utterance of deep import or wisdom; an opinion or declaration regarded as authoritative and infallible; undeniable truth." So, what is at stake here is not the acceptability or even the accessibility of the oracle, but its wisdom. Now, who judges an oracle to be wise? Or, is this question irrelevant, since all oracles are by definition wise—supported by or expressing divine wisdom—and that is what makes them oracles as opposed to mere threats or promises made by one individual to another?

Thomas Malthus, for example, could "fit" the definitions of an oracle, for his principle of population was predictive and had the authority of scientific data and terminology. But, was he indeed an oracle? Was he both wise and infallible? According to Allan Chase:

> Malthus was not, as modern mythology would have it, a simple country curate to whom God had imparted a Divine Revelation about population as His humble messenger went about his pastoral chores. Malthus was, rather, a sophisticated dabbler in political economy, who was well aware that history had long since disproved his great "discovery" that man's ability to produce babies will always exceed his capacity to grow enough food to feed them. If this famous Malthusian "Law" had indeed ever been true in England, it was, thanks to the Agricultural Revolution, no longer true at the time Malthus was born. (Chase 1980, 75)

Malthus was an oracle in the sense of being an esteemed individual whose "words" carried weight, and whose predictions became important public concerns. Malthus could not be ignored; he was too visible and well-connected to be ridiculed or dismissed. But what about Malthus's utterances made them so powerful?

Malthus received a critical review in his entry of the *Encyclopedia Britannica* (11th edition, 1910), so critical, I guess, that the article does not identify its author, an unusual step for most entries, especially since the leading scientists of Europe were enlisted to compose the entries of this excellent edition. The entry states that "it remains a matter of some difficulty to discover what solid contribution he [Malthus] has made to our knowledge, nor is it easy to ascertain precisely what practical precepts, not already familiar, he founded in his theoretic principles." So, why was Malthus a celebrity of his time, a man whose principle drew extensive attention that led to policy debates for years to come? The anonymous author suggests that Malthus' "doctrine is new not so much in its essence as in the phraseology in which it is couched."

Malthus' status, then, is attributed to his linguistic technique, the terms and phrases he used, and the way in which he constructed an old and well known argument against subsidies for the poor. Just as the methodological debates concerning political economy and statistics in Section F of the BAAS turned out to be debates about the uses of language—the proper language of science as opposed to the inflammatory language of economists—so the debate about the Poor Laws or about moral propriety turn out to be debates where linguistic use and technique become paramount. The anonymous critic of Malthus gives an example of how Malthus manipulated his linguistic arsenal in order to push for a certain policy. He takes the sentence "population has a tendency to increase faster than food," and contends that in this sentence population and food are both "treated as if they were spontaneous growths, and which, on account of the ambiguity of the word 'tendency,' is admittedly consistent with the fact asserted by Senior, that food tends to increase faster than population." In short, Malthus became an oracle because he used words and sentences in magical ways, in technical ways that made trivial conjectures appear as insights or that added enough ambiguity to the data at his disposal to ensure the support of his own argument.

The question of language reappears in one form or another whenever oracles are mentioned. Oracles must speak, for otherwise they remain too remote to affect their surroundings; but they speak unlike the rest of us, for otherwise they would no longer be considered oracles. Once an individual realizes this point, it is possible to move from the position of an enlightened individual who has something (urgent) to say to the position of an oracle. It is possible to manipulate the circumstances of one's deliberation and pronouncements to make them appear as if they were uttered by oracles. But is the posturing "as if" one were an oracle in and of itself problematic? Perhaps the way to answer this question is by noticing that the potential for abuse is tremendous, for the public cannot suspend judgment of the oracle until a prediction is or is not fulfilled. In the time gap between an utterance and its fulfillment the oracle reigns supreme—and that situation, as the example of Malthus illustrates, allows an oracle to talk of moral conduct and other public policy issues regardless if they turn out to be at all relevant to the "scientific data and argument" that were issued to support these issues.

Galton's case, as discussed in chapter 1, can be perceived in a similar manner to Malthus', even though the notion of oracle was not introduced there. Galton can be perceived as an oracle warning against the dangers of poor scientific scholarship and the misappropriation of scientific tools and techniques, an oracle whose authority remained unquestioned throughout his professional life, and an oracle whose power had almost immediate consequences when it was used against an individual or a group.

Malthus' example, almost a century prior to the Section F incident, has two thousand years old roots and continues to influence the way contemporary society thinks about scientists as oracles. When appeals were made to oracles in ancient Greek society, in the Judeo-Christian tradition, or in the time of Shakespeare, the appeal was to something or someone who was regarded, as the *OED* reminds us, as "A vehicle or medium of divine communication." Biblical prophets always licensed their visions and imagery in terms of divine inspiration; they were, so they claimed, the vassals of a power beyond themselves, a power that forced them to speak and not one they could ever manipulate themselves for their own benefit.

Being a Biblical prophet did not endear one to the people, and prophets routinely tried to escape God's missions, as the incident of Jonah illustrates. Prophets had a mission, one they often were reluctant to carry out, for it included "bad news" and "threats" that could have turned their kings or their people (not to mention foreign people) against them personally. In a word, there was a risk involved in being a messenger of God: to forestall or avert the message, the messenger would be killed.

When Socrates appeals to the oracle of Delphi, for example, his appeal is twofold. On the one hand, the appeal is to "an unimpeachable authority" (*Apology* 20e), an authority carrying enough cultural weight to validate anything that is said, even something as outrageous as Socrates is the wisest man in all of Greece. On the other hand, for Socrates the oracle can and does, in fact, "sanction" something that is either said or done, it validates, permits, and justifies an activity, a mode of thinking, a particular behavior (*Laws* 3.686a). The "reason" one would take such validation seriously is because of the "wisdom" and "infallibility" that define and frame the oracle. The "authority," then, is a "legitimate" one, and not one won in battle or by sheer force. It is an authority an entire society, presumably, can appreciate, acknowledge, and abide by. It is not an authority—for example, that of a political leadership—that will be continually contested, overthrown, and revised in accordance with the changing tastes and moods of the people, those same people who by definition have no claims to wisdom and infallibility. Instead, it is an authority that transcends the political and economic power structure and relies on "eternal" wisdom and truth. Oracles' power may be deemed a means to an end or only a temporary stage towards the "real" power of gods and nature; but since the access to gods and nature depends on oracles, their power is tantamount to the power of gods and nature.

But, as can be seen in "The Merchant of Venice," Shakespeare has Gratiano play with the notion of oracle to show Antonio that perhaps too much has been made of this notion:

> There are a sort of men, whose visages
> Do cream and mantle like a standing pond;
> And do a wilful stillness entertain,
> With purpose to be drest in an opinion
> Of wisdom, gravity, profound conceit;
> As who should say, 'I am Sir Oracle,
> And when I ope my lips, let no dog bark!'
> O my Antonio, I do know of these,
> That therefore only are reputed wise
> For saying nothing; when, I am very sure,

If they should speak, would almost damn those ears,
Which, hearing them, would call their brothers fools.
("The Merchant of Venice" I.i. 88–99)

Shakespeare's Gratiano is nobody's fool! Are oracles indeed worthy of the status rendered them so far in history? Are they not merely pretentious individuals who believe in themselves and therefore make others believe in the wisdom and gravity of their words? Shakespeare finds it incredulous to let oracles rely on their "reputed wisdom" without "proving" their mettle, explaining why they deserve their reputation and power. Once challenged, forced to speak plainly and explain themselves in unambiguous manner, these oracles would sound like "fools."

It is possible to conclude from these references that having oracles is tantamount to having guardians or shepherds, divine or earthly overseers who can steer society in the "right" direction and give it the "right" answers to all its questions. The certainty with which oracles make their pronouncements relies on divine knowledge and not the partial and uncertain knowledge commonly attributed to human beings; their "wisdom" is divine as well, it is the wisdom only gods possess. And here, once again, the question of responsibility appears in a different guise. Can oracles be held responsible for their utterances, since they are supposedly merely conveying someone else's words? The answer to this question depends, to a large extent, on whether one perceives the "choice" of oracles to have been made by gods or by society. It seems to me that though oracles claim to have what Max Weber coined a "calling" or "vocation," their calling is in fact the product of social solicitation. Oracles are cultural *products*, and therefore hold a peculiar position vis-à-vis the question of responsibility.

If one assumes that oracles are chosen by gods and not humans, then how are the insights of the gods translated and presented to human beings? From the religious perspective the answer is simple: meditation, contemplation, and purity of thought. An oracle is "responsible" when the "translation" and "presentation" come as close as possible to the divine word. The secular perspective is suspicious of such a view, for meditation, contemplation, and purity of thought do not guarantee divine revelation or even an understanding of "nature."

Apparently the question of communication or re-presentation was deemed unimportant and even trivial in the past. When an oracle spoke in riddles, the onus of translation and even interpretation rested unquestionably with the audience. The audience could not and did not dare challenge the oracle for an explanation—if one failed to understand the truth revealed in codes and symbols, it was one's own fault. This situation may seem unreasonable or even unfair to a modern or postmodern reader, yet it is a situation one can easily detect today in the interaction between students and teachers at the highest levels of education. When a passage of a text is assigned to students, they are required to explain and interpret it as best they can—the burden of analysis and reflection is always put on them and not on the passage itself and its author, the one (or many) who have encoded a thought or an idea. The teacher can also evade the problem by claiming that the "author" must have meant something and therefore the "text," no matter how opaque, contains some "truth" worthy of knowing. It is especially worthy of knowledge when the text is a published book or an article in a professional journal, that is, a text whose status has been sanctioned by the intellectual leadership through a process of refereeing its worthiness.

Yet, situations in which a reader is asked to confront a text and know it are not always intimidating; they can motivate an audience, listeners, viewers, and readers to try themselves to participate in the activity of interpretation. A teacher or messenger or oracle, then, becomes a moderator, a relatively passive participant in the exchange that evolves between a text —written or spoken— and those encountering or confronting it. The interpretation of oracles, for example, just as any other interpretation is itself knowledge, a process by which data are examined and discarded, judged worthy or worthless, without ever fully settling the score permanently. Whether one speaks of interpretation in Socrates' sense of recollection or in Nietzsche's sense of an interpretation of an interpretation, the process as a whole is continuous and constitutes knowledge. Oracles and scientists, experts and specialists, are only points along a line, conveyors of a never-ending assembly line of knowledge claims and their verification or falsification.

Grigor, in the film *Quintet* (1979), explains his powerful role in his society as being "only the interpreter of the rules." His job, he says at another point of the film, is "to keep the game alive." It is neither his "judgment" that counts nor his "interpretation" of the entire "game" that starts or terminates the process, the game. Instead, there is a game—a life—that is played, a game the rules of which change over time, being constantly forsaken and revised. Just as "knowledge" in some fantastic way is "there," the game is there, the rules are there, but the "meaning" of the game and its rules are open to a multiplicity of interpretations. Without interpretation, the rules would lose their status vis-à-vis the game, and the game itself would no longer be considered a game, a framework within which certain "moves" or interpretations are permitted and others are forbidden.

Now, is Grigor an oracle, a wise man whose words and statements are infallible, or is he an interpreter? Posed in this way, the question suggests a dichotomy between an oracle and an interpreter so that they cannot be one and the same. But, of course, an oracle can interpret, and an interpreter can provide oracular answers, devised in ambiguous language, or simply be wise. If the dichotomy is relinquished, then an oracle can and often is indeed an interpreter. But, an interpreter of what? According to Greek and Judeo-Christian culture, an oracle delivers—perhaps interprets—divine wisdom. As such, the interpretation is needed in order to have access to otherwise incomprehensible "divine" signs and symbols. But what if there is no such thing as the divine, neither gods nor goddesses?

Asking a question about the very foundation of religious beliefs and sentiments or a question that does not presume an entire ontology of divine beings is itself a novel proposition, a proposition, one can claim, that became palatable only in the so-called modern era. Questioning ontology or metaphysics became palatable because divine beings were replaced with scientific laws and principles. That is, the *content* of the ontology and metaphysics was changed, but the very *existence* of an ontology and a metaphysics that are "beyond" or that constitute a foundation was left intact. So, when the question: but what if there is no such thing as the divine, neither gods nor goddesses? was raised, it could be dismissed as anachronistic, and answered quickly: it does not matter! For nothing is at stake if there is no god, since it is possible to equate, as Spinoza did, God with the World or Nature and thus what is at issue is now "nature" about which we wish to have greater knowledge.

As human beings who are part of and live in the world, the questions commonly raised to oracles are questions about ourselves, our future and well-being and not questions about divine entities. For if humans ever cared about the well-being of the gods it was only in terms of how they would affect them as, for example, in Greek mythology. Oracles were supposed to foretell the future so that humans could survive and even escape their fates; they were expected to reveal the secrets that lay "behind" the world, secrets to which only gods have access. So, whether divine or secular, the quest to know the unknown, or in John Dewey's words "the quest for certainty," remains an important psychological determinant of how humans lead their lives and interact with each other (Dewey 1960).

At this juncture two interrelated issues arise. Why is it important for humans to know the unknown? And, with what certainty must they know the unknown? These two questions and other questions derived from or related to them, the first concerning the connection between epistemology and psychology and the second about degrees of certainty and comfort, guide the discussions in the next two sections respectively.

III: EPISTEMOLOGY AND PSYCHOLOGY

When presented with the question: which came first, the chicken or the egg?, most listeners smile a bit, thinking quickly to themselves that this is a trick question, and that in order not to fall prey to the ridicule intended by the interlocutor, they should remain silent. But the question is not a tricky one, only one the responses to which are both correct, thus undermining the apparent dichotomy or choice given in the question. If one is an "evolutionist," then the egg came first; if one is a "creationist," then the chicken came first. The answers, then, are predetermined by a philosophical framework one chooses or toward which one feels intellectually and emotionally committed prior to answering any question, the present one included.

The choice of being an evolutionist or creationist is not an idle one in the United States, where the Scopes trial is still part of the collective memory, and where the question of the separation of church and state is still debated. So, when speaking of "knowledge"—whether of the origins of life or any other "natural" or "social" phenomenon—one must carefully choose or at the very least be conscious that one is in fact choosing between these two and many other alternative worldviews. For if one is a committed creationist, then at some preliminary level of discussion all psychological characteristics, for example, are attributable to a divine "maker" or "creator" in whose image, as the Bible tells us, humans were created. As such, humans' psychological shortcomings or failures and advantages or successes are intimately connected with divine purpose, divine predetermination, or divine foresight. When questions of "free will" are introduced, they, too, are already bound by a framework that presupposes divine intervention or the suspension of such intervention. On the other hand, if one is a committed evolutionist, then all knowledge claims are historically bound even if some are deemed more fundamental and less susceptible to change than others. Psychological characteristics are considered natural as opposed to divine and are viewed as evolving over time, corresponding to changes in the environment.

Choosing the evolutionist framework in general still leaves room for making or committing oneself to additional choices relevant to one's view of the psyche. It is common to speak of "nature versus nurture," of one's natural psychological tendencies and propensities and those acquired during early childhood socialization. On nature's side, one argues for a fairly stable and unchanging psychological foundation that explains one's behavior at any given moment in one's life. On the other side, one argues for a developmental appreciation of the external conditions and their effects on the individual's well-being or sickness. Moreover, at what level of "selection" should the evolutionary process be understood? If it applies to the species as the "unit of selection" among a variety of species, then it is possible that individuals would not be affected at all during long periods of time; if the process of selection applies to individuals within the species, then one would expect more rapid changes to be discernable over time. The difference between the unit of application—species or individuals—makes a difference in viewing psychological tendencies and inclinations.

The choice between evolution theory and creationism can be debated on epistemological grounds, where empirical evidence is gathered, and where the technique of argumentation is used. As an epistemological choice, the choice is between two sets of standards of knowledge, one secular and scientific, the other religious. But the epistemological choice is a psychological choice as well—psychological in a loose sense—for there is a personal "comfort" or "anxiety" that accompanies the choice. If God is the creator, then the ultimate responsibility is his/hers; if God is not our creator, then there better be order in our evolution so that we know what to expect next. Though affecting individuals' psyches, the choice is not merely personal, for it is influenced by tradition and habit, by fashions and fads that overtake and shape a culture at different times.

Cultural differentiation seems a minor factor in the ongoing human desire to have an ordered universe, according to Ernest Gellner. Epistemologically there is always a choice between "order" and "chaos"; but Gellner documents anthropologically a uniform tendency to prefer order to chaos for personal, cultural, and social purposes. A belief in order, whether traced to a deity or to the laws of reason, has been a human preoccupation for centuries across cultural and geographical boundaries. Oversimplifying greatly, it seems that humans need to uphold a view of the universe that is systematic and organized, explicable and predictable (Gellner 1974). And, as Peter Winch contends, the frameworks we construct are culturally bound, whether they are called magical or scientific (Winch 1964).

The continual concern to order one's world expresses itself differently in light of changing historical contexts. The religious "ordered" worldview has been replaced by a secular evolutionary one on supposedly epistemological grounds, some of which have characterized the modern era or the era that began with the scientific revolutions of the sixteenth and seventeenth centuries, and the shift has been undisturbing psychologically. If anything, the shift has solidified the harkening after an ordered environment. But what does it mean to be an evolutionary thinker? And how does an evolutionary worldview influence one's psychology? Or, how does one's psychological tendencies influence one's preference for an evolutionary perspective? Stephen Jay Gould's version of evolution theory is called "punctuated equilibria" (Cf., Gould and Eldredge 1977). In broad philosophical terms, the punctuated version of evolution differs from the classical version attributed to Charles Darwin insofar as it challenges the "gradual—step by step" and "progressive" direction of evolution. Unlike the gradual development, from a "lower" to a "higher" level, from a "worse" being or situation to a "better" one, where a *telos* is presupposed even if its point of arrival or termination cannot be foreseen, punctuated development is haphazard and nonlinear. There are "leaps" and "jumps," some explicable and some not, all of which are somewhat accidental, contingent, and nonrepeatable.

One may wonder why Gould's proposal was and still is not fully accepted by popular perceptions of evolution and even by some within the scientific community or why there is some "discomfort" concerning this proposal. One explanation, given my insistence on personal psychological propensities, may be the following: according to the Darwinian version it is possible to reconcile the creationist and evolutionist positions and frameworks, for the evolutionary *telos* can be understood to have been predetermined by a divine being so that the beginning of the evolutionary development can easily be attributed to that being. Rhetorically, then, one can ask: does God, as Einstein is reputed to have quipped, play dice with the world?

According to the Gouldian version, a reconciliation between a religious and a secular view on the origins of the species may be untenable. What is imputed to the evolution of the world and more specifically to that of the species is a somewhat chaotic past and history that may never become orderly or predictable. From this perspective, it is "frightening" to think of ourselves as possibly an extinct species or a species whose origins are unclear, not to mention the possibility of applying these concerns to different "units of selection" (Cf., Shanahan 1990), such as individuals, considering the unpredictable nature of each person's life. While Darwin's version is almost as comforting (but not enough for many till today) as the Biblical story of origins, for both explain "categorically" the past and predict the future, Gould's version is worrisome.

At some psychological level, whether the discourse used to explain ourselves is religious or secular, there is a connection between what we know—epistemology—and what we *want* or care to know— psychology. The story of evolution is only an example that enhances the move in the history of ideas from oracles to scientists. The story of human evolution is a story people care about not only because it provides a wonderful scientific schema that explains and predicts but also because it affects them in a personal way and informs the way they think about themselves and those with whom they come in contact. There are direct ramifications to the view of evolution in terms of how individuals lead their lives and how they organize themselves in groups and societies, as can be illustrated in the works of some social Darwinists (Hofstadter 1955). One would expect, for example, that in a teleological evolutionary worldview, individuals would care about the consequences of their actions and how their behavior affects others, while in a punctuated evolutionary worldview, individuals would more likely discard future consequences of their actions because the future is unpredictable and therefore they may venture to behave "irresponsibly" (assuming for both cases individuals as the units of evolutionary selection and development).

The story of Section F of the BAAS, as recalled in chapter 1, also exemplifies the connection between epistemology and psychology. Though the debates about the scientific status of political economy and statistics were carried out in methodological and epistemological terms, though they were bound by the discourse of "science," these debates had an emotional charge; they provoked anxiety and relief, anger and frustration. The attack on the validity and credibility of Section F was no idle intellectual duel, but a forceful attack that meant to have an effect: pain, shame, even conquest. Section F was under siege with the prospects of being publicly humiliated and thereafter dismissed from what was then considered a prestigious scientific community, almost as prestigious as the Royal Society of London. The personalities that were involved in the incident were not engaged in a theoretical dispute the outcome of which could be left open to a majority rule or the rule of the scientific leadership. To some extent, the possibility of changing or transforming Section F from a less to a more qualified section was not proposed at the debates about its future membership at the BAAS. Instead, the individuals who confronted each other in the "trial" were vindictive and hostile, they had something at stake; they all wanted to win in a battle they initiated themselves. The epistemological slope ended in a psychological ravine, so that the distinction between the two became unrecognizable. Jealousy and rivalry, personal gain, and psychological gratification were as important components of the debate about the methodology of political economy as any others. From my perspective, then, to view the incident of the 1870s retrospectively without considering these personal and psychological factors would be a grave oversight, but an oversight that is itself sanctioned by the discourse of "science," where objectivity and neutrality are deemed tenable and valid.

It seems that to talk of epistemological "discomfort" sounds peculiar, while to talk of psychological discomfort sounds reasonable and understandable. It also seems a heresy to confuse epistemology—the discourse of intellectual inquiry and scientific research—with psychology—the discourse of personal feelings and individual growth. "Mixing" the two discourses is considered until today by most philosophers of science a heresy because it robs science of its special status, a status that even its critics are bound to "respect" (Cf., Longino 1990). But if one infuses terms commonly associated with the discourse of psychology into the discourse of epistemology, interesting parallels appear, parallels that may have interesting explanatory powers concerning human inclinations toward certain modes of thought or belief.

For example, in addition to using the terms truth and falsehood in regards to epistemological claims—such as, "it is false that the sun will not rise tomorrow"—one could use the terms scary and disturbing or comforting and safe. The statement about the sun not rising would then appear as: "it is false, scary, and disturbing that the sun will not rise tomorrow." From this revised statement one can appreciate its status: though it may be true under some bizarre conditions—for example, a meteoric rainfall of extremely high density and proportion hitting either the earth or the sun—it remains false (in the sense of a high level of probability) that the sun will not "rise" or appear to humans from earth in a regular rotation of about twenty-four hours. This situation, given these and many more qualifications, is comforting and reassuring to humans who make such statements or who are worried about the truth-value of such statements.

Once understood psychologically (again, in a loosely defined sense), epistemological claims from distant places or distant times would no longer seem as incomprehensible as they do when compared to contemporary (epistemological) discourses that are conditioned by modern science and technology. Moreover, one could reevaluate on psychological grounds, for instance, Winch's anthropological application of Wittgenstein's insight concerning linguistic games and their rules (Winch 1958). When so-called witch doctors and shamans use an epistemological discourse that is difficult to translate into our own, they use a discourse interlaced with or interwoven into a psychological discourse and one that makes perfect sense in its contextual setting. The translation need not be limited between a "native" and a "western" epistemology, but could simultaneously be between a native epistemology and a native psychology, and those two native discourses could in turn be translated into the two western discourses of epistemology and psychology, now opening a set of four translations where before there were only two.

Witch doctors and shamans do not use words such as epistemology and psychology, discourse and translation. Nevertheless, as oracles they cannot pronounce "verdicts" in a context-free environment; instead, the contextuality of their pronouncements, one that includes the psyches of those surrounding them—those who look up to them or critically watch for their mistakes—conditions what they know and what they will therefore say, that is, their sense of the real and the language appropriate to describe it (Winch 1964). To understand oracles, whether our own or those of different cultures, requires a cultural perspective large enough to incorporate at the very least both epistemology and psychology. Whether oracles are called "witch doctors" and wear feathers or are called "scientists" and wear white robes makes no difference to their cultural position. Regardless of their attire and "presentation," they gain their position in society because they perform a dual function commonly associated with oracles, that is, saying something with a great deal of authority about a particular event as if that event is certain to occur and at the same time connecting the event to the people, delivering a message to an audience that has a set of expectations.

How do these individuals, call them oracles or scientists, come to know the expectations of their audience? One way of answering this difficult question is by observing that they are highly sensitive and perceptive students of their culture, studying the history of their culture and its salient characteristics. Being immersed in their culture licenses oracles to practice their trade: they know what would be acceptable or unacceptable, what would increase their status and prestige and what would decrease their popularity. In this sense, then, oracles and scientists are performers who care about their audience and cater to the expectations of their culture (no matter how enlightened or misguided). For example, the modern posture of objectivity and value-neutrality is adopted by scientists because they know that their culture values and respects this attitude toward one's pronouncements, even though scientists may acknowledge privately that they work on low temperature conductivity, for instance, because that is where funding is easily attainable.

But oracles and scientists as performers also suffer the consequences of their performance if that performance is not well received. If the audience expects an ordered universe, for example, in a manner supported by the Bible, the Catholic Church, and Ptolemy, an interpretation that presents a universe in a different manner may be unsettling and even provoke violent reaction, as was the case with Galileo. It does not matter that one "order" is replaced with another; what matters is that the order one learns to take for granted is being challenged and overthrown. Histories of science mention two incidents of "scientific heretics" who stood by the "truth" and were punished for their integrity, Bruno and Galileo. Giordano Bruno was burned at the stake by the Inquisition in 1600, and Galileo Galilei was sentenced to life imprisonment in 1633.

Did the Catholic Church force on the public a certain worldview that required a specific celestial order and hierarchy, or was it merely responding to a public quest for order and certainty? That the Catholic Church had a particular worldview to propagate and protect goes without saying; that its worldview is the most appropriate given its interpretation of divine revelation is also clear from the Church's perspective. But to what extent is the success of the Church in convincing the public to follow its interpretation exclusively attributable to the Church's own teachings or to the public thirst for authoritative and conclusive verdicts concerning human destiny and the fate of the earth remains unclear. Just as the success of oracles and scientists depends on the reception they receive from the public, so does the success of the Church depend on the willingness of congregations to adopt a particular vocabulary or discourse.

Bruno, as Frances Yates tells us, provides an interesting example of an attempt to bridge between religious and scientific ideas and discourses, even though he is commonly perceived to have been a scientist *par excellence* whose scientific dedication led to his eventual demise. Yates' interpretation of Bruno's case does not support the "canonical" interpretation, since she emphasizes the magical roots of his thought and the influence of Renaissance magic on developments in science and technology (Yates 1964, 244). Bruno's commitment to the Copernican perspective and later to his view of an infinite universe with innumerable worlds almost in an Einsteinian mold is understood emotionally and psychologically, not in terms of the emerging scientific methodology of Baconian induction and experimentation. In Yates' words:

> . . . the impulse towards the breaking down of the old cosmology with heliocentricity may have as the *emotional impulse* towards the new vision of the sun the *Hermetic impulse* towards the world, interpreted first as magic by Ficino, emerging as science in Copernicus, reverting to *gnostic religiosity* in Bruno. (Yates 1964, 156, emphasis added.)

According to Yates, a certain religious excitement, having to do with the rediscovery of lost ancient Egyptian texts, brought about a renewed fascination with magical techniques that eventually led to a changed attitude toward the universe—from contemplation to involvement and operation—that transformed epistemological frameworks as well. Bruno, then, takes over the Copernican edifice of mathematics and reintroduces into it prescientific divine mysteries. (Yates 1964, 155)

Bruno, as Yates pictures him, reverted back to an oracular time, when divine revelations were the secret domain of a few select individuals. Bruno the scientist of contemporary textbooks is in fact "the preacher of a `new philosophy' which he expounded in Protestant England and which was . . . basically Hermetic." (Yates 1964, 184) As a "preacher," Bruno has no patience for the Oxford doctors with whom he debates the Copernican view. He calls them "grammarian pedants" who "do not understand philosophy, and who demonstrate their literary frivolity by quoting an Erasmus adage about madness at him when he insists that the sun is at the centre and the earth moves." (Yates 1964, 167)

Bruno's own discourse is passionate. Unlike the Oxford dons he is not concerned with grammar or with quoting the "proper" authorities on science. On the contrary, though advocating Copernicus' ideas, he scoffs at his narrow interpretation and explains that Copernicus' vision was overshadowed by his mathematics. In Bruno's words:

> . . . for being more a student of mathematics than of nature he was not able to penetrate deeply enough to remove the roots of false and misleading principles and, by disentangling all the difficulties in the way, to free both himself and others from the pursuit of empty enquiries and turn their attention to things constant and certain . . . *The Nolan* . . . has released the human spirit, and set knowledge at liberty. . . . Behold now, standing before you, the man who has pierced the air and penetrated the sky, wended his way amongst the stars and overpassed the margins of the world, who has broken down those imaginary divisions between spheres— the first, the eighth, the ninth, the tenth or what you will—which are described in the false mathematics of blind and popular philosophy. (Yates 1964, 236–237 emphasis added designates Bruno's name)

Bruno chides Copernicus for not going far enough beyond his mathematical calculations, not "seeing" what his heliocentric worldview "means." Bruno, with great self-praise and self-confidence, congratulates himself for "saving" Copernicus' insights and being able to "see" how they relate back to divine insights that were originally presented as part of the Hermetic tradition. Bruno's discourse is not scientific in the ordinary sense of the term as established in the mod-

ern era: it is too emotive and poetic. Scientific discourse does not conceive of scientists as angels who find themselves "amongst the
stars," but as laboring individuals who experiment and calculate. But
Bruno's discourse bridges the epistemological and the psychological: "new" knowledge of celestial rotation has an emotional impact
and revives emotional tendencies that may lay dormant for generations because of a particular epistemology that is "blind." Just as
Bruno perceived himself to have understood what Copernicus could
not have understood mathematically, he also perceived of himself as
being able to discern deeper meanings in the "discovery" of the
compass by Mordente: "a hieroglyph of divine truth, a hieroglyph of
the return of Egyptianism, mysteries which were hidden from the
poor, Oxford pedants." (Yates 1964, 295)

For Bruno there was no epistemological significance divorced from
psychology. Whether the psychological is also religious, as in the case
of Bruno, or not, does not change the interesting connection that I
am trying to reconstruct here between epistemological and psychological discourses. In any case, Bruno's religiosity is itself suspect
in the eyes of the Catholic Church, for his indulgence in magic and
the Hermetic tradition was considered profane and anti-religious, so
much so that he was burned at the stake. As Yates argues, Bruno's
condemnation was not due to his scientific and philosophical heresies because they could not be separated in his own thought and
works from his other theological heresies (Yates 1964, 355–356). But
even Bruno's case does not fully answer the question about the
psychological factors or conditions that influence and are influenced
by a certain epistemological model.

IV: A PSYCHOLOGICAL IMPERATIVE

A psychological imperative in the context of the present discussion
is not an imperative in the Kantian sense, but instead a plea to consider in psychological terms what is always considered in epistemological terms alone. In interweaving the epistemological and
psychological discourses, a reader would be free to listen to the psychological anxiety of a storyteller or another listener, regardless if the
story is about witches or nuclear substructures, about political
economy or the rivalry between scientific leaders. A story, then, or
more precisely, "my story," is an invitation and not a front. Since my
story is anecdotal, it must remain provisional and hypothetical in a
way that invites response in the forms of other stories about my story
or about the stories I retell. In a process of narrative reconstruction
the debate itself—whether about authority or about expertise—
rather than a specific outcome is what makes the debate interesting.

The process of deconstruction and reconstruction is a process wherein the "telling" and the "listening" to the narrative become indistinguishable, where the one displaces the other without either "taking over" or becoming dominant. When a text is published, of course, the process is truncated, even paralyzed, since the reciprocity undertaken in the shared experience of exchanging ideas is unavailable. Yet, one may attempt to overcome the limitations of a published text either by using computer technology, which allows an interchange, or by performing the role of writer and reader all the time in the form of a spoken dialogue. A dialogue carried out in a text is directed by an author, who limits the possibilities of exchange as the dialogue unfolds. For example, the Socratic dialogues have been criticized for not being dialogues at all, for Socrates leads his interlocutor to say exactly what he expects him to say, as in the case of the slave boy who "recollects" his geometry in the *Meno*, rather than say something unexpected and thereby catch Socrates off guard.

A dialogue, according to Michel Serres, includes two interlocutors who "are in no way opposed, as in the traditional conception of the dialectic game; on the contrary, they are on the same side, tied together by a mutual interest: they battle together against noise." As the two interlocutors are "on the same side," they "*suppose a third man and seek to exclude him*; a successful communication is the exclusion of the third man." A successful communication is a "battle" "to produce a truth on which they can agree," and not to retain any disagreement (Serres 1982, 67). A dialogue, in this view, is an ordered and orderly process of interpretation that leads to an agreement, where external influences and interruptions are excluded. But not all dialogues must be Socratic, nor need they be limited in a way that ensures agreement and precludes unforseen possibilities and inventions.

The dialogue I try to carry out here is one in which an epistemological voice or perspective has to interact with a psychological one. The conversation of this chapter continues the conversation of the previous chapter and will have something to do with conversations carried out in subsequent chapters. The conversation is "grounded" in a story about an incident that took place over one hundred years ago in Britain, but this grounding is temporal. That is, one must remain skeptical whether or not my rendition is accurate or explores all the possibilities that the "facts of the matter" present; there is also no reason to believe that other stories about the same facts cannot be told; and finally, there is no pressure, only the power of suggestion, to agree that the story told in chapter 1 has any relevance to my story about oracles or about scientists as oracles or about the status of oracles and scientists.

V: POSTSCRIPT

On what grounds, then, should one agree with my assertions or the arguments presented here? To what authority should one appeal? Since the discussion here is about authority, the appeal to authority, and the status of authority, it would be self-defeating to appeal to "another" authority for fear of an infinite regression (Ormiston and Sassower 1989, Ch. 5). But if there is no grounding to what is being said, why should one listen to it at all? In some respects, this question lies at the heart of this book. The answer, therefore, is extremely simple from one perspective, and quite complicated from many other perspectives. From one perspective, one that I feel most at home with right now, one should listen to anything or anyone in a provisional manner, that is, with a great deal of reservation and a critical attitude.

And here, once again, there are two interrelated issues to mention, first, the "story," in Lyotard's sense (Lyotard 1984 and Lyotard and Thebaud 1985) and second, the "listener." The story and listener as reader parallel the difference and connection set forth in regards to epistemology and psychology. Just as the epistemological is fraught with psychology so that questions of truth or validity depend on personal levels of comfort or anxiety, so the status of a reconstructed narrative depends on a mode of persuasion. In other words, the context within which an epistemological debate is examined or a story is interpreted must be broadened to include psychosocial factors. Instead of speaking broadly about the cultural context in which this or that debate is taking place, instead of referring to a context that is itself contextulized from the perspective of those proposing its boundaries, the context I refer to is at once personal and immediate.

The immediacy of the context, the personal and subjective elements that enter into its construction, is itself suspect for those concerned with truth and validity, for it does not offer a "scientific" way of speaking about a situation, describing a state of affairs, or examining potential changes in how things are or are claimed to be. Since the context itself is perspectival and is selected for a specific purpose, a reconstruction cannot pretend to be objective. So, when I narrate a story about Section F of the BAAS or about oracles, I reconstruct the narrative in my own way, expecting the reader to acknowledge a certain level of credibility—conceding at least that reading my narrative is worthwhile. To pretend that what I write is either exclusively mine or shared by everyone else is of course overstating either case.

Does it mean, then, that any story—whether told by oracles or experts—can only be trusted so far and not more, that it should never be fully trusted? Yes. The history of science, as a series of narratives bound to their contextualized constructions, provides numerous examples of discarded and replaced narratives whose truth was fully accepted at some point in history. But a lack of trust or a continued critical sense of mistrust is not necessarily detrimental to one's appreciation of a narrative. On the contrary, a reconstruction avoids becoming a dogma when it lends itself to a multiplicity of readings, when, as Nietzsche contends, its content remains elastic enough for a multiplicity of interpretations and its potential remains forever inexhausted (Ormiston and Sassower 1989, Ch. 4). Unlike a narrative that is interpreted repeatedly, a dogma dies when it ceases to obtain the institutional support that rendered it a dogma to begin with. For this reason the Catholic Church reminds its flock annually (if not weekly) how to behave and how to read its sacred texts and follow its institutional injunctions.

Since my reconstruction draws on certain historical anecdotes and uses them to fit a certain argument or point of view that I find most appealing by comparison to others, I have the latitude to use other narratives to prop it up. For example, I can sporadically use the data of anthropology, behaviorism, and experimental psychology in order to explain what I take to be the connection between epistemology and psychology. But such propping is always liable to draw fire from disciplinary connoisseurs who would like me to use more of their data, rely more heavily on what they take to be "uncontested truths" that they "discovered." But if I quoted their data and referred to them as "stories," they would be outraged for they differentiate between "stories" that are fairy tales and their "scientific reports" to which they assign truth value.

A scientific narrative usually uses a style different from the styles used in other narratives and this amplifies the distinction between its content and the content of other stories. Style is connected to content, the one "molding" and "protecting" the other, so that in their combined articulation they present a unified entity. A scientific narrative is considered to have a different, and for most people a preferred status (on epistemological grounds) than a literary one. Since the "status" is different and presents itself differently, its "reception" is different as well. In its "protected" form of presentation, a scientific narrative guards itself from the sort of psychological traumas permeating literary and artistic narratives, where excitement and horror, for example, are supposed to be part and parcel of the presentation.

One quick reference that can explain my concern with the content/style of scientific literature is the cinema, whether used for explicit pedagogical purposes or for viewing by the general public. The story of nuclear disasters is seen differently in *The China Syndrome* (1978) than in Environmental Protection Agency pamphlets; the story of how babies are "made" is portrayed differently in Woody Allen's film *Everything You Always Wanted to Know About Sex (But Were Afraid to Ask)* (1972), and in the lessons provided by a school nurse or obstetric professional journals. Are the "facts" different in these presentations or is it just a difference in presentation? I would argue that the difference is across the board, that the different presentations also focus on different facts or on different aspects of the situation. A process of interpretive selection is operable at all levels all the time.

Given this long set of disclaimers about truth and scientific validity, what consequences concerning the question of responsibility can be articulated? One may claim that the "relativist" position adopted here is so wide open that it loses any credibility or conviction and is therefore irresponsible. Another may claim that if the author is not convinced of the credibility of a narrative s/he (re)constructs, why should anyone else feel the responsibility to (re)interpret the narrative or design an alternative one? From a clearly defined epistemological discourse these responses make sense and provide "good reasons" for reading this book no further. But a decision to stop reading right now is informed and conditioned by a particular psychological "nerve." When labeling this book "relativist" and "skeptic," a reader is in effect saying: I do not like to read an indecisive book or a book that does not clearly define its commitment to the truth, and moreover, I do not want to take on the responsibility of interpreting this book because I am not sure its author has been responsible at all.

This book is about many things, depending on what focus is given to a chapter or a section, and depending on what prejudices a reader brings into it. One of the things I examine in this chapter is the relationship between a culture and the oracles it sanctions and between culturally designated oracles and their audience. Saying that humans have a need to know their past and future and therefore appeal to divine or scientific oracles may explain a psychological imperative contemporary society must learn to live with, but this still does not say enough about the epistemological validity that ought to be given to what oracles or scientists say. In a similar fashion, saying that the epistemological foundation of any pronouncement, scientific or divine, is necessarily flawed may alert contemporary society, but this still will not convince the public to disregard oracles or not to appeal to them anymore. So, on practical grounds, why raise critical questions about oracles and scientists?

First, a critical evaluation of certain phenomena is a first step toward making judgments or recommending a different approach to a situation. The very choice of focus, in this case on oracles/scientists, is a judgment, a selection that is guided by certain commitments and convictions, an attitude and an orientation. Choosing to look at scientists as oracles, and tracing the notion of oracle in its various historical instantiations, helps approach the situation of scientists as experts or specialists who have a privileged position in our midst. A historically informed reconstruction helps put a situation into perspective, admittedly one that is carefully chosen, but one that allows a critical interpretation and reinterpretation.

Second, once scientists are perceived as oracles, their pronouncements would have the same dubious status as that of ancient oracles: they may be wise and even right in their predictions, but they may be vague and wrongheaded. If the statements of scientists are rendered the same status as those of oracles, then questions of empirical grounding or mathematical accuracy may become tangential and not the focus of a critique of their judgments. One is tempted to address the specific techniques and tools used by scientists to express their views (as in the case of statistical techniques of the 1870s) as opposed to the underlying principles or the general orientation that guides scientific work. For example, does it matter if a scientist is religious or politically conservative for the kind of results that will be produced?

Third, critiques of scientific achievements are commonly divided into two categories. On the one hand, there are those who critically evaluate the great successes of science, the concrete applications in technological terms. There has been a long tradition of pointing out the hazards accompanying every scientific and technological achievement, from pollution to invasion of privacy. On the other hand, there are those who critically evaluate the methodological apparatus used by science and the empirical foundation on which it is based. Attacks on this or that method of inquiry are routine in scientific circles, where one method is preferred to another for specific reasons. For example, the debates between the inductivism of the Vienna Circle and the hypothetico-deductivism of Karl Popper and their continued reverberations in the present illustrate this point. So, the "critique of science" is not new.

But instead of interpreting such critiques only epistemologically, I recommend to look at them psychologically as well. In this context, it may become clear that one may not want to "do away" with science and scientists, nor that one would like to "change" the status granted them. Yet, it may be possible to challenge the view that scientists "deserve" their status for their epistemological sophistication and instead show that scientists remain in a "lofty" position because the public wants this to be the case. Scientists, then, are public servants whose status is at the discretion of the public. Just as the public appeals to scientists, scientists must appeal to the public for good-will and unwavering financial support. The reciprocity of the relationship may not change the relationship, but it will help guard or prevent potential abuses by scientists (e.g., Sassower 1991a). For example, political economists in Section F perceived themselves to be public servants (unlike their counterparts in other sections of the BAAS!) regardless of their putative scientific status and therefore felt responsible for settling the mill strike. If they could not help in this fashion, what good was their theoretical apparatus and the mathematical techniques they so eloquently employed?

Fourth, from a postmodernist viewpoint there is an "explanation" of why scientists are the chosen oracles of the twentieth century in the western world (e.g., Lyotard's). But this explanation is not a legitimation, and therefore clears the way to suggesting other "chosen" oracles. If we agree that the public needs—psychologically—oracles, then there may be a wider variety than scientists. Moreover, other oracles might be even more effective in providing the sort of psychological reassurance that the public craves. For example, filmmakers, playwrights, composers, and musicians, are just as eloquent as scientists in predicting the future, warning against disasters, and promising new adventures.

CHAPTER 3

Scientists as Experts

I: INTRODUCTION

Just because humans are inclined to listen to others in order to make up their minds does not mean that any oracle will do. The selection of oracles is historically informed, and a historical narrative can show how the choices of Greek society influenced the choices reflected in the constitution of the BAAS and the eventual threat to expel Section F. The dichotomy of philosophers and sophists in ancient Greece, for example, has given rise to a preference of philosophy over sophistry to the extent that philosophical arguments and positions are preferred to mere sophistry—the dichotomy gave rise to a hierarchy. While philosophy was thought to employ rigorous, scientific methods of inquiry (called "dialectics" by some), sophistry was aligned with poetry that was thought expressive and imaginative, worthy of those interested in twisting arguments to suit their purpose, with no regard to the standards of truth established by philosophy or the methods of inquiry deemed appropriate for the pursuit of wisdom and truth.

Setting dichotomies of disciplines or of methods of inquiry, demarcating between discourses, is a way not only of setting up hierarchies but also of explaining and justifying the privileged position of expertise. The etymology of "expertise" shows that there is a difference not only between experts and non-experts, but also between theoretical and technical expert "know-how," where the theoretical level is more important than the practical (no matter how they are respectively defined). In tracing the traditional dichotomy (and hierarchy) of philosophy and sophistry, making use of Jean-François Lyotard's perspective, I attempt to show that dichotomies turn into hierarchies.

Though the pragmatics of dichotomies—their usefulness for particular purposes—is not in dispute here, I wish to argue that when the pragmatic ceases to be paramount in the evaluation of the *temporal* validity of dichotomies, one may find an alleged *permanent* validity in their subsequent hierarchical ordering. For instance, while Section F was almost dismissed from the British scientific community because it presumably failed to fulfill the criteria supporting

54

theoretical expertise—considered better or superior to practical expertise—it did manage to accomplish something in the way of practical expertise—resolving a strike dispute. In light of this situation, one may question the very criteria by which theoretical expertise—if expertise can indeed be demarcated from other forms of knowledge—has been judged not only on its own grounds but more specifically in terms of its preference or superiority over practical expertise.

This chapter ends with an exploration of a different way of thinking about expertise: instead of philosophically justifying or legitimating expertise, one should recognize that expertise is nothing more nor less than the ability to replicate past successes and modify past failures. In this respect, then, the success of Section F in resolving a strike dispute counts far more—pragmatically speaking—than the use its members made of newly codified mathematical and statistical techniques. Technical expertise emerges in a new light, without the need (in terms of credentials and academic paraphernalia) for theoretical pretense, shield, or disguise.

II: PRESENT PRAGMATICS

Lyotard claims that "Postmodern knowledge . . . refines our sensitivity to differences and reinforces our ability to tolerate the incommensurable. Its principle is not the expert's homology, but the inventor's paralogy." (Lyotard 1984, xxv) Lyotard expresses here an attitude that is characteristic of postmodern knowledge, an attitude that explains how the incommensurable remains incommensurable, no matter what one attempts to do about it. This attitude toward the incommensurability of knowledge-claims explains that the multiplicity of theories and practices or language games is irreducible to any single set of principles or rules, unless one considers the tolerance of incommensurability to be a principle/rule as well. The inventor's "paralogy"—Lyotard's or ours—allows for "mistakes" or incomplete ideas and models of thought; it promotes openness and linguistic experimentation; it condones not having conclusive and permanent answers to the questions of the day. Lyotard's "task," then, "is one of multiplying and refining language games" (Lyotard and Thebaud 1985, 49). If there is any implicit recommendation here, it is one that encourages one to be willing to participate in the activity of multiplying language games (i.e., discursive practices and techniques), however one defines that activity. Multiplying language games is in itself not an easy task, for Lyotard does not talk about mere repetition, but about being inventive, creative, and playful. And the refinement of language games is open-ended as well, for no set criteria of refinement are provided, no guidelines that stipulate "this is better" or "this is more accurate." If anything, the refinement, according to Lyotard, is a piecemeal work, a "case by case" process (Lyotard and Thebaud 1985, 28–29, 73–74) that takes its cues from the context in which it unfolds. For Lyotard, then, the "enterprise of experimentation on language games" (Lyotard and Thebaud 1985, 49) is not a way to "supply reality," but instead, a way to "invent allusions to the conceivable which cannot be presented" (Lyotard 1984, 81).

Lyotard entices his readers to "experiment" and appreciate a multiplicity of discourses none of which need be discarded nor privileged over another; yet, he still works out his own views in terms of dichotomies, where one set of statements seems preferable to another. A critical review of Lyotard's posture is not undertaken in order to distill an "inconsistency" between his "theory" and "practice," for (logical) inconsistency may be irrelevant to Lyotard's experimentations. So, to find Lyotard, or for that matter anyone else who is interested in linguistic experimentation, "guilty" of violating "rules" openly disclaimed is itself "inconsistent." Instead, this is an attempt to *use* Lyotard's discourse or language game to examine the broad issue of the possibility of dispensing with—once and for all?—dichotomies. *This* use of Lyotard is experimental as well, a way of thinking about a problem through the practices of Lyotard without much concern if his attempt is or is not successful in using/dispensing with dichotomies. In this respect, the notion of success is contextualized, and therefore no logical inference from the success/failure of another to my own can be made.

Just as the hierarchical structure of the BAAS is questioned in chapter 1, I wish to examine here the broad issue of the possibility of dispensing with dichotomies that lead to hierarchies. I acknowledge from the outset the difficulty of dispensing with dichotomies, since the very quest for "dispensing with dichotomies" sets a stage whereby there is in fact a dichotomy between dichotomies and non-dichotomies. As I hope to illustrate, the quest for dispensing with dichotomies may remain elusive or become a heuristic device, for the language game of dichotomies is quite useful for articulating a situation that discounts dichotomies. Besides, one can uphold temporarily certain dichotomies for specific purposes, regardless if they correspond in any sense to "reality" or to some truth. So, the issue is not to rid our discourses from dichotomies because all dichotomies are inherently "evil," but rather to differentiate between—again, a dichotomy of sorts—the language of dichotomies that helps or that obstructs the achievement of particular purposes.

Conceiving of (scientific) knowledge as a multiplicity of language games none of which is more important or fundamental than another requires a different attitude from a public (not to mention the scientific community itself, as seen, for example, in the attitudes of the leadership of the BAAS) accustomed to a *hierarchy* of language games or models of knowledge. Once the public sets pragmatic parameters, appeals to experts and specialists would be deemed less important for the sake of deciding on public policies for at least two reasons. First, as Lyotard says, because no longer can there be a presumption legitimating the "expert's homology," and second, because no obvious, cognitive limits would be presented and accepted, only blurred boundaries between one narrative and another. The effects of such an intellectual "gestalt switch" would be psychological as well, similar to the linkage of epistemology and psychology in chapter 2, for individuals will be seduced to participate in the activities of their society and not remain passive observers.

III: A LANGUAGE GAME OF DICHOTOMIES

A language game of dichotomies has one fundamental rule: every set of ideas or objects can be divided into two (or more) groups so that one group is clearly demarcated from another. The demarcation itself can follow any number of criteria, depending on intellectual commitments and fashions, but what remains similar in all cases of demarcation is that the criteria themselves are explicit and open to examination. Though explicit on one level—stating what they are— the criteria remain elusive to further scrutiny—why are these the criteria and not others? At this ancillary level of scrutiny, the criteria are "fixed" as the foundation or basis on which the rest of the discursive edifice is established, and the criteria become a set of convictions whose authority is seemingly beyond reproach; they are at the origin, at the beginning of the game.

"Modernity"—in its Enlightenment or Frankfurt guise—justifies the adherence to rules that set dichotomies. From this perspective, if criteria were forever open to challenges and revised continuously, the entire edifice would fall apart and complete anarchy would stand in the way of attaining Truth. Every demarcation would have to be accepted (and abandoned) since no final or ultimate appeal would be possible, as the appeal to "rationality" has been made. That is, the entire activity of demarcation—what science is expected to accomplish—would become futile. The appeal to a foundation would be amorphous and useless: how can a game have rules at all if their very articulation is in constant flux?

By contrast, the postmodern condition (one that could be found already within modernity, Lyotard 1984, 79–82) agrees that demarcations are convenient discursive moves, even necessary at times, because of the sheer magnitude of data that contemporary society encounters. This agreement suggests an appeal to a set of criteria by which one set of statements or linguistic games is conveniently separated from another, but does not condone the choice of criteria or their "eternal" usefulness, because it differentiates between the appeal to criteria and their validity (however defined), between pragmatics and truth. Appreciating the temporal authority of a set of helpful criteria and demarcations differs from licensing them permanently. So, acknowledging that the rule of demarcation—the game of dichotomies—is pragmatic, open to changes and revisions depending on specific contexts of practice, preempts any reliance on a single set of foundations forever.

The dichotomy just set above between modernity and the post-modern condition is itself not rigidly observable, for it, too, is a demarcation of convenience, undertaken in order to illustrate a point of view, an opinion, a concern, and is not meant to "reveal the truth" in any absolutist manner. Besides, such a dichotomy highlights a difference, it does not underscore a preference.

This is the case especially since most dichotomies established in the history of ideas do not recognize their original purpose, whatever that may have been. For example, when one recalls the Greek dichotomy of philosophers and sophists, one commonly presumes—given the canons of the history of Western ideas—that one group, philosophers, are seekers and lovers of the truth and therefore are enlightened and socially responsible individuals, while the other group, sophists, are manipulators of language and therefore irresponsibly sell their *techne*.

Using a historical case study, I attempt to show that in order to understand Lyotard's notion of "postmodern knowledge" and the role of pagans in producing and disseminating it, and in order to explain my engagement with his view—and its relevance to my view of expertise—it is important to reevaluate the status of the dichotomy of philosophy and sophistry.

IV: PHILOSOPHERS AND SOPHISTS: A DICHOTOMY?

A "sophist," according to the *OED*, is "In ancient Greece, one specially engaged in the pursuit or communication of knowledge; especially one who undertook to give instruction in intellectual and ethical matters in return for payment. In the latter sense, contrasted with philosopher, and frequently used as a term of disparagement." This last comment, regarding the negative connotation associated with sophists undermines a neutral attitude towards sophists, one that also defines them as individuals who are "distinguished for learning." In many ways, sophists are just members of an alternative group of "wise or learned" philosophers. But the negative connotation overwhelmed the neutral so that the definition of sophist is most commonly rendered as "one who makes use of fallacious arguments; a specious reasoner."

Plato/Socrates (or just Socrates for brevity sake) was single-handedly responsible for undermining the status of sophists so that they would be considered dangerous swindlers who charged money for their intellectual services and used their skills to debate any issue with fallacious arguments (Kerferd 1981, Ch. 1). These two issues, payment and fallacious reasoning, are the standard behavioral characterizations that have haunted sophists and relegated them to a debased status warranting public contempt.

Though Socrates emphasizes the difference in *method* and *approach* between him and sophists, it seems that he lay the emphasis purposely on what may be perceived as superficial reasons (on "the sophistic movement," see Rankin 1983, Ch. 1). There is no perceptible difference between the *behavior* of sophists and philosophers like Socrates: they all use rhetorical and oratorical skills and techniques to debate a point or convince another person or a crowd, and they all charge fees for their services, no matter in what form these fees appear (Rankin 1983, Ch. 2). However, some argue that there is a radical difference in what each group takes to be knowledge, its principles, attainment, and purpose (Cf., Rowe 1983, 421–424). From this perspective, then, it seems that Socrates was concerned with the challenge to his view of knowledge posed by sophists and wanted to marginalize and thereby silence them once and for all.

As an important voice and authority, Socrates based the dichotomy of philosophers and sophists on the characterization of sophistry as "a hunt after young men of wealth and rank" (*Sophist*, 223b) that results in "the manifest ruin and corruption of anyone who comes into contact with them" (*Meno*, 91c). Although the odium toward these men is both blatant and obvious, Plato's dialogues never quite give specific arguments against this supposedly dangerous group. Though various characterizations are interspersed throughout the Platonic edifice, there are no "substantiations," or at the very least, examples of how the sophists were in fact corrupting young minds or manipulating principles of "truth" as opposed to the "teaching" in which Socrates was engaged (Kerferd 1981, 4–5).

For example, in Plato's *Sophist* we find the following characterization of sophistry as:

> The art of contradiction making, descended from an insincere
> kind of conceited mimicry, of the semblance-making breed, derived
> from image making, distinguished as a portion, not divine but
> human, of production, that presents a shadow play of words—such
> are the blood and lineage which can, with perfect truth, be assigned
> to the authentic Sophist (*Sophist*, 268c).

However, it is possible to argue that the description of authentic
sophists as those engaged in the art of contradiction-making could
also fit Socrates who is considered to be a dialectician. The description of image-making can fit sophists and philosophers alike, as one
recalls the numerous images and myths reproduced in the
Symposium or the *Republic*. Conceited mimicry is not the exclusive
domain of sophists, as Socrates' cynical ridicule of his "prey" interlocutor shows time and again. And finally, play of words is something
Socrates was accused of in his own trial, and therefore could not have
been the preoccupation of sophists alone.

If there are great similarities between the philosophical *form*
displayed in the activities of both sophists and philosophers, then the
difference traditionally attributed to these groups must have something to do with the *content* of their art (e.g., "relativism" in sophistry,
see Bett 1989). Whether the dichotomy of philosophers and sophists
is based on content or form, it may be useful to consider one of
Hegel's observations on the matter:

> Sophistry is certainly a word of ill-repute, and indeed it is partic-
> ularly through the opposition to Socrates and Plato that the
> Sophists have come into such disrepute that the word usually
> now signifies that, by false reasoning, some truth is either refuted
> and made dubious, or something false is proved and made plau-
> sible. *We have to put this evil significance on one side and forget
> it*. (Hegel 1974, I, 354, emphasis added)

Lyotard would be in agreement with Hegel's observation, since for
Lyotard the dichotomy set up by Socrates privileged philosophy and
discredited the contributions of sophistry. It was a dichotomy that
turned into a hierarchy, instead of one that provided multiple
choices. Lyotard does not quarrel, as do some contemporary scholars who attempt to "rehabilitate" sophistry (Kerferd 1981 and
Rankin 1983), with the dichotomy of philosophy and sophistry.
Accepting the dichotomy—but rejecting the traditional hierarchy—
he imagines the contributions of sophists as well as those of what he
calls "pagans" alongside those of philosophers.

Once sophists and pagans are granted a status similar to that of
philosophers, their different discourses can still be distinguished but
can no longer be placed in a hierarchical order. From Lyotard's per-

spective, sophists and pagans may react differently to this situation than philosophers might: they will welcome the multiplicity of language games in which their own discourse is one of many, while philosophers will still be concerned with ordering discourses and wishing their own to be privileged. As will become apparent below, if Lyotard's own perspective is paralleled with that of sophistry and paganism, then it is possible to appreciate the difficulty of dispensing with dichotomies and with the "urge" to order discourses and narratives in hierarchies.

V: LYOTARD ON SOPHISTRY AND PAGANISM

According to Lyotard, postmodernism is an experimentation with a pragmatics that "for some Sophists, is a decisive aspect of the poetic: It is true that the poet is not concerned, after his statements are made, to enter into a dialogue with his readers in order to establish whether or not they understood him." (Lyotard and Thebaud 1985, 5) Unlike the Platonic dialogue that attempts to reach Truth, even if it is limited to a truth of consensus among the participants in a dialogue (Lyotard 1988, 23), poets and sophists do not care to reach the Truth or even reach a consensus. Instead, the sophists recognize that their language games could not be permanently grounded because these language games are of a "society of gods that is constantly forced to redraw its code." (Lyotard and Thebaud 1985, 17)

Given that the grounding of language games—discourses, narratives, stories, and arguments—is in the hands of "gods" who have their own obscure code and that the code is redrawn constantly, Lyotard agrees with the sophists that "knowledge"—of the divine code or of anything else—is inherently incomplete and context bound. It is knowledge similar to that of the oracles and scientists, as discussed in chapter 2, knowledge that gives dubious support to claims of expertise. In his words:

> There is no knowledge of practice. One cannot put oneself in a position of holding a discourse on the society; there are contingencies; the social web is made up of a multitude of encounters between interlocutors caught up in different pragmatics. One must judge case by case. (Lyotard and Thebaud 1985, 73–74)

Epistemological contingencies—within "knowledge of practice" as Lyotard says, or understood more broadly by me to include *all* knowledge—denote "an absence of unity, an absence of totality." (Lyotard and Thebaud 1985, 94) The sophists, then, would conform to Lyotard's postmodern motto: "Let us wage a war on totality; Let us be witnesses to the unpresentable; Let us activate the differences and save the honor of the name" (Lyotard 1984, 82; see also Lyotard 1988, 44).

Without a totality, one is left with only "a patchwork of language pragmatics that vibrate all the time. And that means that the partners, the people who are assigned their roles by the language games in which they are caught, occupy positions that are incommensurable to each other." (Lyotard and Thebaud, 1985, 94) The absence of a totality in and of itself does not signal a problem, since the different language games may all "fit," thus presenting no conflict with one another. Yet, since there are always "different pragmatics" or a "differend" as Lyotard calls it (Lyotard 1988), interlocutors can (and in fact do) find themselves at times in incommensurable language games or multiplying language games. In light of this situation, Lyotard describes the "patchwork" of judging case by case.

Lyotard's sophistry, especially in its connection to a "society of gods," is also paganism. Pagans are not atheists, but rather believers in gods not only as forming "a society" but more importantly as the "authors of narratives." Since human beings "are not the authors of what they tell . . . of what they do," "they must constantly match wits with the fate that they have been given." (Lyotard and Thebaud 1985, 36) The human "fate" or the "postmodernist condition" is the abandonment of the classical/modernist promise of a firm grounding or a Truth that is permanent and reassuring. Paganism, therefore, is "the acceptance of the fact that one can play several games, and that each of these games is interesting in itself insofar as the interesting thing is to play moves. And to play moves means precisely to develop ruses, to set the imagination to work." (Lyotard and Thebaud 1985, 61)

A postmodernist, a sophist, and a pagan, are all matching their wits with one another in a diversity of discourses that reflects no loyalty to a single language game or a single set of metaphysical rules. For them, no language of dichotomies, for example, can ever retain its authority or remain forever unaltered, as, for example, was the expectation of the leaders of the BAAS. From their perspective, then, the dichotomy of philosophers and sophists has outlived its usefulness. As Lyotard illustrates in his own case, some of those involved with the postmodern condition figured out a "new move" for this age-old dichotomy of the Greeks, a new use through which to explain what differentiates postmodernism from modernism (not in a "periodizing sense" (Lyotard and Thebaud 1985, 16n)). "Pagans," as Lyotard says, "are artists . . . [who] can move from one game to another, and in each of these games (in the optimal situation) they try to figure out new moves. And even better, they try to invent new games." (Lyotard and Thebaud 1985, 61) But has Lyotard, who may be considered by some to portray the characteristics associated with pagans, in fact invented a new game or figured out new moves?

VI: LYOTARD'S LANGUAGE OF DICHOTOMIES

Claiming to find this theme among several sophists and rhetoricians, Lyotard distinguishes between "statements that narrate or describe something and statements that prescribe something." Moreover, when one moves from descriptions to prescriptions, "there is a change of language game." Lyotard uses the dichotomy of descriptions and prescriptions in order to emphasize that while descriptions are grounded empirically, the language game of prescriptions—applied by him to justice and law—is flexible, "without criteria" (Lyotard and Thebaud 1985, 17).

In a similar fashion, Lyotard, following Aristotle whom he considers a sophist, distinguishes between knowledge and opinion where the former presumably belongs to descriptions and the latter to prescriptions. As he says: "with respect to all these matters at least [politics and ethics, that is, prescriptions], we are always in judgments of opinion and not in judgments of truth." (Lyotard and Thebaud 1985, 28) Lyotard, in spite of his paganist orientation, still believes that there is truth about certain narratives and not about others: while descriptions have a scientific basis, prescriptions do not. In other words, in the case of prescriptions alone "there is no metalanguage, and by metalanguage, I mean the famous theoretical discourse that is supposed to ground political and ethical decisions that will be taken as the basis of its statements" (Ibid.), while descriptions constitute presumably a "scientific theoretical discourse."

Even if one agrees with Lyotard "that one of the properties of paganism is to leave prescriptions hanging, that is, they are not derived from an ontology," and that "one cannot derive prescriptions from descriptions" in a Kantian sense, it is unclear to what extent Lyotard retains the dichotomy of descriptions and prescriptions along "classical"—as opposed to his own—lines of demarcation, where a hierarchy is immediately imposed (Lyotard and Thebaud 1985, 59). One would expect that whatever sophists and pagans have to say about rules and criteria in the interplay of language games, narratives, and stories, would not be confined to one set of statements but would be applied to all statements whatsoever.

If "we are always within opinion, and there is no possible discourse of truth on the situation" (Lyotard and Thebaud 1985, 43), as Lyotard claims, then his acceptance and use of the dichotomy of descriptions and prescriptions as a dichotomy of knowledge and opinion respectively can be understood as a heuristic device. But for what purpose? Is it not in order to demonstrate the impossibility of philosophizing without dichotomies? Yet, such a realization does not license the establishment of hierarchies.

Lyotard almost says as much, but not explicitly. If Lyotard insists that "one is caught up in a story," then the story might include both descriptions and prescriptions and therefore their difference along ontological lines may be blurred. If anything, contemporary astrophysics as well as folklore illustrate Lyotard's own contention that we are "immanent to stories in the making, even when we are the ones telling the story to the other" (Lyotard and Thebaud 1985, 43).

From my perspective, it seems useful to play with dichotomies in order to illustrate a point, emphasize an issue, or set up a way to change the rules of language games. It also seems useful to recycle an age-old dichotomy for a particular purpose, so that the recycling alters the dichotomy in some sense. For example, there is no reason to shield empirical descriptions or scientific statements from the same interpretive apparatus, where one must judge case by case, commonly applied to so-called nonscientific statements and theories. If interpretation rules over all language games, then it should be applied equally, regardless what specific form the interpretation takes. In this respect, too, the latitude illustrated in the activities of the BAAS economists—both their choice of subject matter for research and their practical application of their principles—can be perceived as an interpretive move, a move with suggestive power for other scientists of the BAAS. A move, therefore, that would simultaneously challenge the hierarchy of the BAAS sections, the notion of science, and the authority of experts.

VII: THE MYTH OF EXPERTISE

Lyotard's literature includes experts, their activities, knowledge, and the social status accorded to them. Experts are commonly perceived as those best qualified to answer questions concerning their fields of specialty. Since they are allegedly in command of specialized knowledge, it is perceived that they alone are qualified to make pronouncements and decisions connected to their fields. What sort of command of specialized knowledge do experts have? Those who say that experts can make certainty claims regarding their fields are inadvertently perpetuating a myth about expertise—a myth, to be precise, about the certainty claims of experts and not about the obvious fact that there are people who are rightly perceived as experts or who may know more about a certain area than others. It is a myth because the view that epistemological certainty exists—one that ignores inherent margins of error—is untenable.

One of the first to perpetuate the myth of expertise was Socrates, encountered earlier in this chapter as the one responsible for the dichotomy of philosophers and sophists. Charged with corrupting the minds of the youth and with being a nonbeliever and dismayed with charges better suited to sophists, Socrates explained that he was not corrupting the minds of the youth, but instead being an expert in helping those minds acquire wisdom, using an analogy from horse-training:

> Take the case of horses; do you believe that those who improve them make up the whole of mankind, and that there is only one person who has a bad effect on them? Or is the truth just the opposite, that the ability to improve them belongs to one person or to very few persons, who are horse-trainers, whereas most people, if they have to do with horses and make use of them, do them harm? (*Apology* 25b–c)[1]

This illustration was used to command the (commonsense) assent of his jury. It makes sense that only very few are specialists in specific areas who deserve to state the "last word" in their area of specialty. Socrates' argument about expertise provides one of the first formulations of the myth of expertise, a myth about the certainty of the claims made by experts, and therefore about the justified preference—the hierarchical ordering—of expertise over other forms of knowledge.

If accepted, the myth has an immediate pragmatic consequence since it suggests that only experts can and should make decisions about their specialty, and that only experts in the same field may judge each other's decisions. What about non-experts? They seem unqualified to be external reviewers of the decisions of experts, for they do not possess the specialized knowledge that qualifies experts to make certainty claims. In this sense, then, the myth of expertise guarantees, as was seen in the case of the BAAS, that experts judge other experts and that experts are shielded and even insulated from public reproach.

On one level, the situation just described (concerning the evaluation of expertise) makes sense. Some presuppositions about science—certainty and correspondence to reality—to mention just two, implicitly endorsed by postmodernists like Lyotard, provide a convenient foundation on which the myth of expertise remains a description and not a myth. But, on another level, the myth is also a political and social prescription. That is to say, if epistemological concerns have undermined the standard view of science as certainty, there is much room to redraw the social parameters within which experts pronounce their judgments and propose public policies. Since expertise based on certainty can disarm, even disenfranchise, those whose judgment leads them to conclusions different from those legitimated by experts, what remains may turn out to be a power struggle, defined now in economic and political terms and no longer in epistemological or even psychological ones.

VIII: PRESUPPOSITIONS ABOUT SCIENTIFIC EXPERTISE

Views about science depend on a set of beliefs concerning two fundamental features of science. The first concerns the rational basis of all scientific inquiry, and the second concerns the Enlightenment notion that all rational people can easily come to an agreement about every aspect of scientific inquiry (Collingridge and Reeve 1986, Ch. 2). For the sake of brevity I shall only remark here that it is mistaken to narrowly conceive of all of science as based on rationality. There are many nonrational aspects to scientific inquiry—such as the "logic of discovery" or ingenuity, funding possibilities, and the dissemination of ideas and theories—which depend on the social and political setting of a specific scientific community. The history of mathematics, physics, and astronomy during the Middle Ages provides ample testimony for this claim (Cf., on the transmission of theories of vision from ancient Greece by Arab scholars to the Continent, Lindberg 1976), as well as contemporary work in the psychology (Cf., Faust 1984) and the sociology of science (Cf., Latour and Woolgar 1986).

Michael Polanyi and Thomas Kuhn, among many others, have explored the extent to which there are basic agreements among scientists, and the reasons for them. The claim that shared rationality and logical procedures will ensure agreement among scientists is contested with examples concerning the personal dimension of scientific discoveries and experimentations (Polanyi 1958, 1966), the intellectually and compulsive power of the scientific establishment, and the "normal" scientific work contained within a given paradigm (Kuhn 1970).

This is not to say that science as such is irrational nor that scientific inquiry has no grounding in rationality. Rather, the orientation exemplified by some of these scholars emphasizes that nonrational (as opposed to irrational) elements are part and parcel of scientific activities and play an important role in shaping the scientific landscape. These nonrational elements are crucial in determining, for example, which scientific theories or models are taught in schools or which innovative ideas are published in scholarly journals. As mentioned in the case of Section F of the BAAS, individual rivalry and jealousy are unfortunately not absent from scientific discourse (Agassi 1981, Chs. 1, 6, 14).

If one believes that all science is based on rationality and rationality alone, it is easy to believe that all scientists can come to an agreement on all scientific issues. There would seem to be no obstacle to their finding a common road to the Truth. Following this line of argument, one could say that since expert knowledge is based on rationality alone, only irrational people will disagree with experts' scientific views. However, if expert knowledge is understood as specialized knowledge limited to specific areas of inquiry, knowledge which may be mistaken or refuted, then expert judgments are open to repeated scrutiny and criticism according to the context in which they are proposed. Karl Popper's view of epistemology rejects the inductivist attempt to reach certainty and some ultimate Truth about our universe, and instead suggests using the method of proposing conjectures and then trying to refute them. His method never reaches certainty about truth claims, except for the certainty that what has been refuted is no longer true (Popper 1959 and 1968).

The Popperian view of science is in agreement with the so-called postmodernist orientation, but seems much more critical than Lyotard's vis-à-vis scientific statements and discourses. In light of this view, even the expert can only conjecture and provide us with a best guess, never a definitive statement. The myth of expertise, then, is a myth about the certainty of expert knowledge claims. It does not rule out the possibility that there are indeed specialists who know more (practically) about their specialties than the rest of society, nor does it preclude the possibility that heeding expert advice is the most appropriate mode of action in a particular situation. So, an outright rejection of all expert knowledge would be impractical; such a rejection would violate what I consider a useful Lyotardian motto: judge only case by case.

The practical dimension of expert knowledge—the trial of Socrates and the trial of Section F as well—deserves a reevaluation of the epistemological dimension of expertise. The epistemological narrative, as already noted in chapter 2, is always intertwined with a psychological narrative. It is frightening to relinquish expertise just as it is frightening to become too dependent on it. Is there a way out? The Committee on Technical and Scientific Evidence in Courts of Law was formed by the BAAS in 1862. Its findings were quite alarming. The committee reported that in many cases the evidence of experts was contradictory; it confused juries and judges and had even "shaken the credit of professional testimony" (BAASR 1863, 373–74). The committee was of the opinion that expert testimony was valuable in adjudicating both civil and criminal cases, and therefore did not want to suggest eliminating the use of experts in courts of law altogether. So, what could be done about contradictory testimonies of experts?

The committee recommended that "by a legislative act, judges should be empowered, on application from a suitor, in causes of a technical character, to convene skilled assessors, the number of whom should not exceed three, and who should give their opinions truly on the statements of the witnesses" (BAASR 1863, 375). What does this mean? Hegel would have described it as a "bad infinite," for if one set of experts (witnesses) are to be judged by another set of experts (assessors), why not check the judgment of the second set of experts as well? Besides, whose expertise counts more? And what qualifies one expert to judge another? Are academic credentials enough? Does experience count? All of these are primarily practical questions, questions that already concerned the BAAS and are still with us. So much so, indeed, that the talk of the "postmodern condition" still plays a useful role in suggesting different ways or similar ways couched in different vocabularies to deal with the enigmas that expertise presents.

IX: EXPERTISE AND AUTHORITY

The *OED* links "expert" to being "experienced in" or "having experience of," so that an expert is someone who "has gained skill from experience." The experience in question can be either theoretical or practical, in a particular area or in a variety of disciplines. But once skill is gained, the expert is "one whose special knowledge or skill causes him to be regarded as an authority." So, the issue may be less whether or not experience has been gained or a skill mastered, but rather whether or not an alleged expert deserves to be regarded as an authority. Socrates discusses the analogy between midwifery and his role as an educator and a thinker concerned with epistemological questions. But while emphasizing that midwives must themselves have given birth earlier in their fertile years (their experience), he also tells us that he has not "given birth" to wisdom. A midwife is an expert in this framework, for she has specialized knowledge, she has experience, and she is best suited for her task. As the midwife of the soul (rather than the body), Socrates claims to be both an expert like any other midwife and a non-expert because of his disclaimers about his own wisdom (*Theaetetus* 149–151).

The definition of expertise—a dictionary's or a Socratic—would still not resolve the problem posed by the BAAS and repeated into the present about the ultimate or legitimate authority of an expert. The hierarchy of experts is set in Plato's *Republic*, where the super-expert is, of course, the philosopher-king. He can judge all other experts, and thereby give society the final verdict in any dispute. But, as the example of the leadership of the BAAS illustrates, should society license, once and for all, any hierarchy of expertise? (Cf., Agassi 1985, 73).

The question of a hierarchy of experts is simultaneously a theoretical and a practical question, for it reintroduces the question of the myth of expertise in which the issue of epistemological certainty is not doubted. The authority of experts is legitimated by the view that experts are sure about what they say, and that anyone in their position would agree with them. But the legitimacy of the authority of experts must diminish if one recognizes the weak epistemological foundations on which it rests. Is it useful, then, to speak of expertise without permanent, foundational authority?

Though a more comprehensive answer to this question is found in chapter 5, for current purposes one can briefly recall that the traditional answer is no: experts must have authority. Only experts can have legitimate authority, and the philosopher-king is the candidate best suited for having the ultimate authority to rule a society. The BAAS concurred with this view, and suggested legitimating and thereby retaining the authority of experts within their own community. Instead of a philosopher-king having the final word, they proposed a set of scientists-kings whose opinion would have final authority in all disputes (such as Section F) and in all legal cases (a binding authority on juries and judges). These suggestions have not lost their force over the years, so that an examination of the notion of expertise is routinely accompanied by an examination of the notion of authority.

Is there an alternative to the traditional answer to the question of the relation between expertise and authority? If one is willing to suspend judgment about what qualifies as expertise and how to reevaluate the criteria by which expertise is established, then there may be an obvious alternative. For example, one may no longer speak of expertise across all disciplinary boundaries without regard to specified contexts. When this is done, it would be possible to separate expertise into sub-categories for a diversity of responses to expert-judgments and their respective authority. The diversity will be reflected in different mixtures of skepticism, criticism, and rational assent.

One could argue alternatively that society should be highly skeptical of theoretical, scientific expertise, while accepting less skeptically technical expertise emanating from years of experience at acquiring a certain skill to perform a specific task. Scientific expertise and technical expertise are both open to recurrent challenges and refutations, and deserve a skeptical attitude. But since they are both allegedly based on rationality, they also deserve a rational assent if and when they make sense and work. There is also political expertise, the expertise of decision-making within a given social context. This expertise is often perceived to be more personal in nature than scientific or technical expertise, so that it requires an approach different from all others. One could list a different set of sub-categories for expertise, or label differently the ones listed here. But whatever the sub-categories and labels adopted, experts should be approached with a mixture of respect and skepticism, in a word: contextualized expertise is much more useful than a categorical one or one that claims permanence.

X: SELECTING EXPERTISE

As Ludwig Wittgenstein points out, certainty has less to do with the truth than it does with an attitude (in a weak sense) toward what one thinks is true or the impossibility (now in a stronger sense) of not being wrong (Wittgenstein 1969, 2–6). In his words: "Certainty is *as it were* a tone of voice in which one declares how things are, but one does not infer from the tone of voice that one is justified" (Wittgenstein 1969, 6). Not only is Wittgenstein "moving" the epistemological into the psychological but his view lends itself to the position that the search or quest for certainty often indicates a rigidity of mind and refusal to entertain questions and criticism (even constructive criticism). So, if the myth of expertise is exclusively examined in terms of scientific certainty, one may overlook the connection between epistemology and psychology discussed in chapter 2. The question of expert reliability or authority, then, would have to be reintroduced in terms of a societal comfort-level, the socio-psychological conditions under which critical reflection is enhanced or subdued (under coercion or voluntarily).

Psychologically, of course, it is comforting to consult with an expert with specialized knowledge and acquired skill that are based on a great many experiences because this expertise goes beyond the personal experiences of other individuals. Whether or not experts "abuse" their status by claiming certainty where none can be detected may become a moot point, for even their expressions of self-doubt would be readily ignored (and in this respect abused) by an audience that has no knowledge of or experience in a particular issue. Using the dichotomy of theoretical and practical expertise, one could perceive expert judgments to be confined to the solution of technical problems. But how does one define technical problems? Is there a clear distinction between technical and theoretical problems? Besides, once one establishes the category of technical problems, what kind of problems are included?

If one includes all social problems, that is, the problems of mitigating conflicting needs and wants within a specified social and political matrix, as technical in nature, then one would presume that a solution or a set of solutions could be easily constructed. For example, the idea of social outcomes as unintended consequences of private decisions could then be treated by experts as a mediating term between individual and society. Without the prevalence of unintended consequences, expertise in social matters would make little sense. By contrast, if all social problems are understood to be soluble under proper conditions, that is, with the guide of enough specialized knowledge, then society could rationally be "handed over" to its technicians, its experts.

At this juncture one may wish to shift gears, once again, and reintroduce epistemology where psychology may rule. For even if it feels right to let someone else who knows more mediate or even "rule" social decision-making processes, it is not clear that such a feeling would not be radically transformed if experts were found not to have a strong claim of epistemological certainty. In other words, a changing public attitude, a change of heart, would be explicable not only in terms of a fickle public, an emotional mass but also in critical terms of the continuous evaluation of any knowledge claim presented by a group of experts. What, in fact, do experts *know*? Lyotard's response is the following:

> [Y]ou teach what you know: such is the expert. But as the student (the addressee of the didactic process) improves his skills, the expert can confide to him what he does not know but is trying to learn (at least if the expert is also involved in research). In this way, the student is introduced to the dialectics of research, or the game of producing scientific knowledge. (Lyotard 1984, 25)

What surfaces in this formulation is not only a skepticism about the notion of certainty but also a broader questioning of the entire process by which scientific knowledge is produced. As Bruno Latour so aptly illustrates, the productions of scientific facts involve not only professional discourses and laboratory experiments and reports but also a whole engagement of the supporters of science outside the scientific community (Latour 1987). This process, if one wishes to use this term, is one wherein scientific knowledge, in Lyotard's words, "does not represent the totality of knowledge; it has always existed in addition to, and in competition and conflict with, another kind of knowledge, which I will call narrative in the interest of simplicity" (Lyotard 1984, 7).

Once scientific knowledge is paralleled with other kinds of knowledge, the "game of science is thus put on par with the others." Being "put on par" means, at the very least, that the dichotomy of scientific and nonscientific knowledge does not have to turn into a hierarchy (as I think it often does even for Lyotard despite his distaste for privilege). But, in addition, delegitimating the prestigious status of scientific knowledge has the following consequence: "it is incapable of legitimating the other language games. . . . But above all, it is incapable of legitimating itself, as speculation assumed it could" (Lyotard 1984, 40). The question of self-legitimation is important for scientific knowledge and for expertise in order to shield them from the criticism of a "lay" public.

Just as there are problems in accepting Socrates' dichotomy of philosophy and sophistry, there are problems in accepting the dichotomy of science and nonscience. As Lyotard correctly recalls:

> The fact is that the Platonic discourse that inaugurates science is not scientific, precisely to the extent that it attempts to legitimate science. Scientific knowledge cannot know and make known that it is the true knowledge without resorting to the other, narrative, kind of knowledge, which from its point of view is no knowledge at all. Without such recourse it would be in the position of presupposing its own validity and would be stooping to what it condemns: begging the question, proceeding on prejudice. But does it not fall into the same trap by using narrative as its authority? (Lyotard 1984, 29)

If scientific knowledge, and therefore expertise that relies on it, cannot depend on a legitimation from another discourse, must it not rely on self-legitimation? If the answer is yes, what would such a self-legitimating move look like? Here is Lyotard's answer:

> This is how legitimation by power takes shape. Power is not only good performativity, but also effective verification and good verdicts. It legitimates science and the law on the basis of their efficiency, and legitimates this efficiency on the basis of science and law. It is self-legitimating, in the same way a system organized around performance maximization seems to be. (Lyotard 1984, 47)

The circularity of this procedure of legitimation commonly escapes public scrutiny. Why? Perhaps the answers have to do with a long-standing social and political conditioning that has appealed to the public's anxieties and promised to "handle" all (technical?) problems on behalf of the public democratically.

But what if the scientific discourse is nothing more nor less than a set of stories that are routinely "verified" (Lyotard 1984, 60)? Would that way of looking at scientific knowledge change cultural attitudes toward experts? Would the public resist this formulation for fear that there is nothing out there it can take for granted or rely on?

XI: THE LANGUAGE OF EXPERTISE

Speaking to and about the public is much more difficult than speaking to and about a group of experts. While the former may refuse to engage in a discussion of the kind presented here, the latter may find the challenge worthwhile if for nothing else than to refute and dismiss it once and for all. What language game is appropriate for a discussion about expert knowledge? If one participates in the expert language game, one may be co-opted and thus lose a necessary (external) critical edge; if one does not participate in the expert language game, one may not be heard at all for the other language game may be deemed worthless. This set-up may be at the heart of debates that seem to work at cross-purposes, where one group of people speaks loudly but is not heard, or if heard, is not listened to.

Joseph Schumpeter has the following observation about experts and their language, an observation that is at once both internal and external to the particular language game played by experts:

> Those who profess to be engaged in the task of widening, deepening, and "tooling" humanity's stock of knowledge and who claim the privilege that civilized societies are in the habit of granting to the votaries of this particular pursuit, fail to fulfill their contract if, in the sheltering garb of the scientist, they devote themselves to what really is a kind of political propaganda. (Schumpeter 1954, 805)

But how does one draw lines of demarcation between the language of experts and that of propaganda? Is Lyotard, and with him most other so-called postmodernists, correct in claiming that setting propaganda as a lower language game by comparison to the language game of scientists in the hierarchy of language games is inappropriate and even misleading?[2] Though Schumpeter presents his warning in an unqualified manner, it is not quite clear whether or not experts can ever avoid participating in a form of propaganda, that is, a form of discursive expression that is at once awe-inspiring and persuasive. The language of experts is some sort of a "jargon of authenticity," as Theodor Adorno calls it. In his words, the "jargon—objectively speaking, a system—uses disorganization as its principle of organization, the breakdown of language into words in themselves" (Adorno 1973, 7). That is, the jargon distances the audience from the speaker as an oracle, bewilders and overwhelms it at the same time.

Though Adorno's criticism is much more concerned with fascism and the jargon of allegedly authentic nationalism, contrasting it with the language of philosophy, this is helpful here:

> Philosophical language transcends dialectically in that the contradiction between truth and thought becomes self-conscious and

thus overcomes itself. The jargon takes over this transcendence destructively and consigns it to its own chatter. (Adorno 1973, 12)

What is missing from the jargon, according to Adorno, is the critical self-reflection of philosophy that puts into question the very foundation on which its rules rest. As such, the jargon of experts—politicians and scientists alike—

> shares with positivism a crude conception of the archaic in language; neither of them bothers about the dialectical moment in which language, as if it were something else, wins itself away from its magical origins, language being entangled in a progressing demythologization. That particular neglect authorizes the social using of linguistic anachronism. The jargon simply ennobles the antiquity of language, which the positivists just as simply long to eradicate—along with all expression in language. The disproportion between language and the rationalized society drives the authentics to plunder language, rather than to drive it on, through greater sharpness, to its proper due. They don't fail to notice that one cannot speak absolutely without speaking archaically; but what the positivists bewail as retrogressive the authentics eternalize as a blessing. (Adorno 1973, 42–43)

Adorno's complaint is twofold: on the one hand, the jargonized use of a language game becomes anachronistic and petrified, it loses its potential for change, and on the other hand, those using the jargon fail to realize how language-dependent their activities have become, how much their role as experts relies on a certain language game.

One response to Adorno's and even Lyotard's philosophical concerns would be the following question: do you believe that by paying attention to the language of expertise all the problems associated with the social role of expertise would be immediately resolved? That is, does the focus on language in and of itself lead the way toward diffusing social and political implications that arise out of the cultural status given to experts? To some extent, both Adorno and Lyotard would have to respond in the negative, that of course not everything rises and falls in accordance with the level of attention paid to linguistic usage. But that is not the whole answer.

What Adorno reinforces in these few quotes is an attitude one overlooks all too often, an attitude characterized already by Wittgenstein as one that carries with it certain psychological predispositions, wherein one is more readily susceptible to accept or listen to a certain kind of information while ignoring another. As Wittgenstein warns, the language game of "certainty" is one where "doubt gradually loses its sense" (Wittgenstein 1969, 9), where "the *truth* of certain empirical propositions belongs to our frame of reference."

(Wittgenstein 1969, 12) Moreover, Wittgenstein would be in agreement with Lyotard's notion of paganism, saying in reference to the "scientific" language game that "the propositions describing this world-picture might be part of a kind of mythology. And their role is like that of rules of a game; and the game can be learned purely practically, without learning any explicit rules." (Wittgenstein 1969, 15)

The public as well as the community of scientists/experts forgets at times that the language game played in the name of science is only a self-contained language game whose justification remains forever in doubt, and whose rules are not constantly under scrutiny. Once the specific language game of experts is shielded, in Schumpeter's terms, it creates a barrier that is difficult to surpass for experts and the public alike. Language barriers and linguistic codes are integral components of our cultural structure. This much would be agreed upon by all disputants on the question of the language of experts. How much does language matter?

Perhaps language matters quite a bit in the case of experts, since they can be perceived as the carriers of descriptive knowledge (in Lyotard's sense), the translators of that knowledge through story-telling techniques (some quantitative, some not), who cross language games (scientific and nonscientific, for instance). As oracles and ambassadors to another language game, they bring along a message that is at times translated and at times remains incomprehensible. But ambassadors can also make policy decisions, engage in what Lyotard would describe as prescriptions. That is, stories, as mentioned above, are difficult to keep exclusively in a descriptive or pre-scriptive mode; these designations become quickly blurred when an articulation is attempted.

As the next chapter tries to illustrate, it is not only the broad and abstract question of the language game of expertise and its translations that affect cultural conditions and responses to experts. In addition, it is possible to document prevalent disciplinary attitudes towards a multiplicity of expert languages that translate at once into an established hierarchy.

CHAPTER 4

Blurring Disciplinary Boundaries

I: INTRODUCTION

The case study of Section F of the BAAS can be extended and generalized in certain ways so that its particularity does not render it atypical or unusual. The "end" of the story about the BAAS is the beginning of another story, a story that concerns the blurring of disciplinary boundaries. In an age of increased specialization, especially under the influence of organizations such as the BAAS and the AAAS—where disciplines are segregated and ordered within a hierarchy—there has been a recent shift toward general and "grand" theories. Must the blurring of disciplinary boundaries necessarily lead to a grand and therefore "unified" theory? The example of political economy, including the experience of the late nineteenth century, may shed some light on the possible answers to this question.

On the one hand, there is a tendency toward the reduction (in principle or in fact) of one discipline into another. According to the reductionist view, economics, for example, can be reduced to psychology, just as biology can be reduced to biochemistry. The advantage of a reduction is the simplification of an ever-increasing complex network of interrelated disciplines. But such a reduction is dangerous, for it allows a level of simplification that overlooks the subtleties of different disciplines and thereby creates a hierarchy of scientific authority—where one discipline is more "fundamental" than another—in a manner displayed already at the BAAS and discussed in chapter 3 as well.

On the other hand, there is a tendency toward the independence of each discipline in terms of the uniqueness of its methodology or specific content. The advantage of this approach is a freedom of innovation in terms of models for research so that "original" work will develop. But this approach overlooks areas of overlap between and among disciplines so that the insights of one discipline are not utilized even when applicable to another discipline. For example, the complete independence of economic theory would limit its use of cultural and psychological insights concerning the question of individual preferences.

Instead of adopting either approach, instead of playing into another dichotomy, this chapter attempts to hold onto a position that recognizes the interrelations of all areas of inquiry but that does not therefore reduce all disciplines into a fundamental or unified one. Political economy, according to this position, is at once part of natural and moral philosophy and therefore cannot be categorized exclusively as a natural philosophy or a science.

II: APPROACHES TO DISCIPLINARY BOUNDARIES

In an age of increased specialization, there has been a recent shift toward proposing general and grand theories of the universe, or at the very least of the social sciences. When such attempts have been undertaken, they have usually focused on some of the following questions: Do all the social sciences have a common foundation or methodology? Can they all be explained in a similar fashion? Are all the social sciences reducible to one set of principles? In one form or another, answering these questions would require broad brush strokes, what Lyotard calls "grand-narratives." As such, what would be the advantage of looking at once at a variety of fields may be undercut by the disadvantage of overlooking subtleties inherent in any attempt to have an overview of entire fields of research.

One approach to the question of grand-narratives is to abandon any such attempt and remain with the more limited narratives, the culturally defined fields of inquiry as language-games or discourses that have developed over time. This approach may be explained in terms of the impossibility of doing justice or fully accounting for all the fields under consideration when one tries to bring them together, to collect them under one expository umbrella.

A second approach to the questions raised by grand-narratives is to illustrate that grand-narratives are nothing more nor less than narratives of one field in terms of another. Put differently, it is possible (via a grand-narrative) to show how one field of research, say economics, is reducible to psychology, and therefore when talking about economics one in effect talks about psychology. This reductionist approach may be either weak, showing how one field depends on another, or strong, showing how all fields of inquiry depend on a single set of principles (e.g., those of Newtonian physics). The BAAS adopted this approach in setting its hierarchy of the natural sciences. This approach, as already seen previously and as will be discussed in further detail below, has the following distinct characteristics.

First, under the reductionist approach one assumes that fields of research are prima facie distinct or independent from each other so that it can later be proven that they are in fact neither distinct nor independent but rely on each other or on a set of similar principles. In this respect, the approach merely supports its own prejudices or begs the question it raises. Second, this approach sets a hierarchy of fields of research or sciences so that some are more fundamental or basic than others, a way of thinking that implicitly claims that some sciences are preferable or better or at least more important than others. As the case of the BAAS illustrates, this approach reinforces prejudices as opposed to examining alternatives to the social or political construction of the intellectual map.

Instead of accepting these two approaches, it may be more useful to rethink the definitions of fields of research or sciences, so that the approaches mentioned above may be critically evaluated. This third approach may itself become a grand-narrative, bringing together a variety of related fields of inquiry. One would have to argue for a certain set of criteria according to which it is justified to attempt any grand-narrative at all, where a meta-level of discourse is conjured. In what follows, I presume that such an attempt is at once inevitable and valuable, and try to illustrate what such an attempt may look like. My presumption and illustration are open, of course, for further investigations into the validity of such an attempt or another similar to or different from it.

The relationship of psychology and economics serves as a paradigm through which to examine the usefulness or uselessness associated with the three approaches listed above, a paradigm that connects to the examination of economics as part of the natural sciences in the BAAS as well as to the relations of the social sciences themselves as fields of research or disciplines. Psycho-history, social psychology, cultural anthropology, and psychological economics are perceived as subdisciplines or newly founded disciplines that cut across the traditional boundaries of the social sciences. There is some excitement about the blurring of traditional boundaries, an excitement over the possibility of studying a set of problems using the insights from more than one quarter. But, there is an accompanying fear that cross-, inter-, or multidisciplines will adopt a narrow focus of their own. For example, focusing on the relationship between psychology and economics, there is a newly dubbed field "psychological economics" that is a specialized area of research. The research is focused on the attempt to increase the predictive accuracy of economic models of human behavior through rigorous (i.e., mathematical) employment of current psychological principles. This attempt is novel in its replacement of classical views of psychological individualism (that led to a mistaken notion of methodological individualism) with an appreciation of the interdependence of consumer preferences.[1]

Yet it should be recalled that the concern over the relationship between economics and psychology is not recent nor limited to psychological economics as a field of contemporary research. Daniel Bernoulli tried to explain as early as 1738 why people are commonly averse to risk and why risk aversion decreases with increased wealth. That is to say, Bernoulli (credited usually with contributing to the theory of probability, see Todhunter 1865) attempted to connect the psychological notion of risk aversion as it was experienced in gambling situations (but not limited to them) and financial conditions of poverty and wealth (Arkes and Hammond 1986, 195). In addition, Adam Smith's *Theory of Moral Sentiments* and *The Wealth of Nations* are supposed to be directly connected, thus illustrating how he was concerned to account for the connection between psychology and economics (not as separate fields of inquiry, of course, but as areas of research). (More on this issue see below when examining political economy as natural and moral philosophy.) And other social scientists, such as Vilfredo Pareto, Karl Marx, Auguste Comte, Wilhelm Dilthey, and Max Weber, have been concerned to study the relations of psychology and economics, or study both fields as important aspects of a broadly perceived science of society.

In tracing the history of economic thought, one can easily identify specific psychological principles and theories that were employed implicitly or explicitly by economists. In my mind, one could trace the interdependence of psychology and economics, not having to focus exclusively on the more obvious cases, such as the Austrian School, both that of Carl Menger and that of his Americanized disciples. Instead, one could undertake to examine the history of ideas and couple the statements of philosophers, for example, dealing with psychology and with economics so as to show how they perceived the relations of these fields (i.e., indicate consistencies or inconsistencies as the case may be). But instead of trying to couple two sets of statements about allegedly different subjects so as to find a common ground or discrepancies, it is possible to carve out a new area of mutual interest, such as psychological economics.

What is psychological economics? Is it an intersection between economics and psychology? Or, is it an area of research to which both economists and psychologists turn their attention? Alan Lewis, for one, distinguishes between psychological economics and economic psychology: "the former refers to the 'psychologizing' of economics and the latter to the extension of the study of human behavior to include economic behavior." Psychological economics is also understood as behavioral economics, a "more comprehensive economic discipline where economic predictions may be improved" (Earl 1988,

189). The thrust of this intellectual movement, then, is to increase the inductive study of human behavior, instead of continued deductive analysis.

But is such an integration and cooperation easily attainable? Among the skeptics is Randall Bausor who explains that "one difficulty with endeavoring to glean insights for economists from theories of psychologists is that so many distinct psychological theories have attracted adherents" (Earl 1988, 18). The problem, then, is a problem of selection. Rod Cross, for instance, suggests that the problem of choosing between the alternative psychological theories may lead to an infinite regress. He therefore asks: "Would economists not sleep happier in their own beds, and still be able to perform as well in their theoretical tasks, without worrying how to spell psychology?" (Earl 1988, 59) This problem of selection, as Thomas Kuhn would say, has arisen because psychology itself is still in a pre-paradigm stage, and therefore there is no single, well-defined theoretical apparatus to which one can turn. But this, we must agree, is also the situation with economics itself, for it, too, is still in some pre-paradigmatic stage of development in Kuhnian terms.

In addition to the problem of choosing between psychological theories in order to employ them in economics, there is also the difference between the disciplines. One characterization of the difference claims that economics is more likely to deal with system-wide issues and problems, while psychologists tend to have a more limited or narrow focus. This situation has stalled potential exchange and collaboration, as Cross says, because "of the limited gains in content to be had from the trade, especially given the threatened obliteration of content which their existing theories contain with regard to the system-wide implications of behavioral patterns" (Earl 1988, 65).

What is it that economists and psychologists share so that "trading" is possible? At the very least, according to Herbert Simon (Simon 1983, especially 7–35) and Paul Slovic (Arkes and Hammond 1986, 173–193), they share a concern about rational decision-making processes. One can say, with John Hey, that both disciplines as studies of human behavior "share an ultimate aim: to predict human behavior" (Earl 1988, 85). The focus on the predictive aspect of (rational) human behavior and not on its explanatory aspects is because from Comte's time prediction has been one of the most important criteria by which a field of inquiry qualifies to be scientific.

But will a systematic (e.g., mathematical) study enable predictions of human behavior? Many critics of the shift in emphasis from qualitative to quantitative study of economics, such as John Baxter, claim that such a shift is prone to oversimplifications (Earl 1988, 145). Instead, they recommend that we begin to appreciate, among many others, the fact that consumer preferences are interdependent, and as such require the incorporation of psychological principles and theories as exogenous variables in economic models (Mason in Earl 1988, 125, 144). A focus on the individual level will be, then, in terms of the social context in which decisions are made. The integration of psychology into economics necessitates, for example, coming to terms with consumer psychology and escaping classical notions and theories of utility and value (Earl 1988, 160). This is true especially for cases such as conspicuous consumption, as already noted by Thorstein Veblen (Veblen 1899).

III: ECONOMICS AND PSYCHOLOGY: A CASE STUDY

The integration envisioned by the contributors to psychological economics can be successful only if the interdependence of economics and psychology is made explicit.[2] The notion of interdependence is most ambiguous, for it can mean that both fields cannot be separated or that each field benefits from the insights or the development of the other.[3] Moreover, it is difficult in the case of psychology and economics to make an argument for a certain direction of influence based on some historical chronology, that is, that the prior establishment of one field necessarily led to its influence on the field that was established later. Some historians consider psychology as a discipline younger than economics; while the latter dates back at least to Adam Smith (in the eighteenth century) the former is usually associated with some developments of the mid- or late nineteenth century.[4] To others this situation may seem odd since the obvious reliance of economics on psychological principles dates some fifty to a hundred years before the actual formation of psychology as a discipline.

So, how can the relationship between psychology and economics be expressed more precisely? At the very least, these two fields of inquiry seem to have something in common (ontologically) or share something (methodologically), so that they are intertwined in at least four different ways. First, as already noted in the case of psychological economics, one may claim that both fields draw from the same roots or foundations for the construction of their theoretical frameworks. Second, one may claim that psychology relies on economics; third, that economics relies on psychology; and fourth, that the two fields are less interrelated than seems at first. In briefly examining these views, it becomes clear that regardless of the objections raised by the fourth view, the common adoption of the third view is for the purpose of granting economics scientific status (presuming its scientific status as a field of research or discipline).

In thinking about the second and third views, one is struck by the problems associated with the issue of reductionism. There are those who claim that the reduction of one field to another is necessarily accompanied by a loss of autonomy. That is, if economics indeed depends on psychology, can it still be considered an independent field of inquiry? But before drawing some implications that any reliance or claim of reduction has for the case of economics and psychology in regards to claims of scientific credibility, the notion of reduction must be clarified.

To begin with, there is a difference between "reduction" and "reductivism," as Harry Redner argues. Redner claims that there are two interpretations of the concept of reduction, a positive and a negative. The negative interpretation given to the notion of reduction by philosophers such as Nietzsche criticizes and deconstructs inquiry in a manner that leads to an interpretation of science as "nihilistic." The positive interpretation of the Positivists, according to Redner, accepts reduction uncritically and welcomes its accomplishments. Called "reductivism" by Redner, this second interpretation envisions a unity of science such that a full reductivist program will lead to a "literal annihilation of metaphysics" (Redner 1986, 92–93).

The roots of this distinction can be found in the comments of Karl Popper concerning the nature of psychologism as a metaphysical orientation and not merely as a methodological choice (Popper 1959, ch. I, section 2). The distinctive character of reduction, then, is understood not only in metaphysical terms, but also in pragmatic terms. That is, one must ask questions about the purpose of performing a reduction from one field to another, or from one set of categories to another, in order to appreciate the functional nature of such a reduction. Reduction, then, entails no necessary loss or annihilation of any sort, and instead is conceived as an important tool for accomplishing tasks that cannot be accomplished otherwise.

Another way of approaching the issues associated with reduction is to distinguish from the outset ontological and methodological reduction. Using this distinction, one may claim that a methodological reduction has no direct bearing on any ontological claims (of reduction). Just because economics uses the methods of psychology or vice versa does not mean that the laws of economics are the laws of psychology (or vice versa). Once again, practical considerations take precedent in choosing to employ the methods of one field in the course of studying another. These considerations, in turn, are informed by an instrumentalist approach to scientific theories and methods, an approach that portrays epistemological choices in terms of certain metaphysical and ontological commitments.

Finally, it is possible to characterize the relations between economics and psychology in terms of the difference between diachronic and synchronic reduction. Diachronic reduction is usually identified when one science or one set of theories and models is replaced by another so that the replacement becomes the successor science. An argument in favor of a diachronic reduction from psychology to neuroscience is made, for example, by Paul Churchland.[5] Such a reduction eliminates the need for retaining psychology as a field of research, since anything that is meaningful in psychological terms is meaningful at all precisely because it is explained in neuroscientific terms.

Unlike the eliminative posture of diachronic reduction there is synchronic reduction that perceives one field or set of theories as a master-science for other theories and fields of research. Such conception of a hierarchy of sciences was not only proposed by Comte, but was also upheld by the leading Victorian scientists (Morrell and Thackray 1981). This means that economics, alongside sociology and political science, for example, can be subsumed under psychology, where psychology is the master-science. This notion of reduction makes no claims concerning replacement or succession, and instead focuses on some hierarchical ordering of fields of research.

The different possible definitions and uses of the notion of reduction may bring about a confused explanation of the relationship between or interdependence of economics and psychology. The reliance, for instance, of economics on psychology may mean in the strong sense that economics can be replaced by psychology (e.g., that economics is nothing but applied psychology in Wicksteed's terms of 1933); but it may also mean in some weaker sense that psychology serves as a master-science to economics (and other sciences) so that the reliance does not entail the elimination of economics as it is commonly known. From a pragmatic point of view, there is no sense in pursuing any reduction unless it yields results that cannot be reached otherwise. The results themselves are evaluated in terms of their instrumental value, and not as if they reveal the true nature of the world or of human behavior or of economic exchanges.

IV: BLURRING DISCIPLINARY BOUNDARIES

What does it mean to say that both psychology and economics draw on the same foundations? Historically this question received a simple answer: since they were conceived of as separate fields of inquiry only quite recently, it is likely that any ideas associated with psychology and economics were probably linked to the same philosophical school of thought or philosophical orientation.[6] For example, if we discuss the Cartesian era, then we can claim that

Descartes' views concerning the human mind as separate in principle from the body had also something to do with his views concerning the interaction between human beings in the marketplace (not only of ideas, but also of goods and services).

A more recent example is from the philosophical notion of utilitarianism. The philosophical ideas and principles associated with this school of thought have had their impact on psychology as well as on economics. The foundations of the notion of utility is hedonistic in the sense of attending to the individual level of pain and pleasure, of needs and wants, of satisfaction and frustration.[7] Given the prominence of utilitarianism, it is not surprising to view the relationship between economics and psychology as that of two fields drawing from the same source, or building upon similar foundations of a master-principle (as opposed to a fully established master-science).

Economics and psychology, according to this view, are claimed to have been influenced by the same philosophical ways of thinking about people, their environment, and their interaction. For example, the terms frustration and gratification make sense in either field; they require no reference outside of one field and within another. Even when defined differently in either field, these terms remain fixed within their own linguistic frameworks and therefore allow for transposition and translation. We can talk of economic frustration when not receiving enough return for one's investment, or when not getting paid enough for one's work; and we can talk of psychological frustration when a child is not immediately able to satisfy a need for warmth or relief from physical pressure or pain.

Within more specific conceptual frameworks, some like Bausor believe that when neoclassical economists employ psychology, they may find that the two fields feed on each other's insights, their dependence is mutual: "Whereas economic equilibrium may require psychological stability (if not health), understanding the sources of emotional perseverance is of economic significance" (Earl 1988, 31–32). Understanding the relationship between psychology and economics in terms of the use they make of similar or identical terms and phrases remains helpful but incomplete because focusing on terms alone is too broad.

There is another way of perceiving the reduction of economics and psychology to a common foundation. Instead of focusing on the same heritage or tradition—a single set of texts and theories that influence both disciplines—one can define both fields as ideologies. Economics and psychology can be portrayed as ideologies in the sense of providing only partial descriptive views of the individual and the environments in which individuals interact. Though approaching the issue of ideology from apparent diametrically opposed perspectives, both Adam Smith and Karl Marx provide arguments for demystifying the linkage between economics and psychology as if they were separate or isolated areas of research. Smith explains the marketplace not only in economic terms or in terms of self-interest; he adds a general backdrop for making these economic conditions intelligible, describing what he takes to be the fundamental principles that guide the human condition: mutual trust and cooperation. Though leading to a capitalist order, an order commonly understood in terms of a competition that motivates and prevails among individuals who interact with each other, Smith's framework is meant to integrate economics and psychology into one field of study, based on the same basic principles.[8]

Marx is more explicit in his concern for establishing or at least outlining the master-science or the master-foundation that makes economics and psychology attendant frameworks. Marx criticizes the portrayal by classical economists of the free exchange of goods and services in the marketplace as if the creation of wealth and its distribution take place under conditions of fairness (at least in the sense of equal opportunity). In a similar fashion, Marx criticizes the notion of individual mental and physical powers as privately determined and exercised, regardless of social conditions. For both the economic and the psychological perspectives, Marx adds a broader framework that is historically and socially determined. In this manner Marx hopes to overcome the mystifications of either field and provide insights into the human condition and its potential transformation (Marx 1844 and 1887–1894).

V: DISCIPLINARY RELIANCE

The second view of the relationship between economics and psychology maintains that psychology depends or relies on economics. The strong version of this view claims that without economics one cannot make sense of psychology. Put differently, in order to construct psychological theories and articulate psychological principles, one needs to account for economic conditions and principles. Can this view be substantiated?

One attempt to substantiate this view of the relationship between economics and psychology is in the studies of Gary Becker on human capital. According to his view, economics is the field that deals with scarce resources, and as such provides the foundations for the examination of the allocation, distribution, and risk analysis (and involvement) of one's personal life (Becker 1964, 1976). Understood in these terms, then, there is a sense in which psychology, among other social sciences, is reducible to economics. Here the reduction is not limited to methodological issues, but includes ontological assumptions and commitments as well.

Another way of thinking about the reliance of psychology on economics can be illustrated in the case of psychoanalysis. This conception may show, for example, how psychoanalysis is developed and consumed as a commodity, among other competing commodities (e.g., the entertainment industry). Moreover, it is possible to illustrate that the foundation of psychoanalysis depends on the binding financial situation into which therapist and patient enter. Realizing that a therapist is only interested in getting as much money from a patient as that patient can possibly afford to pay and in return is willing to give as little as possible medical advice and treatment helps, according to this view, explain what motivates a therapist to enter a psychoanalytic relationship with a patient. Put differently, realizing that a patient is trying to get away with paying as little as possible for services valued at a high price, helps explain why a patient seeks the psychoanalyst's help.

The foundation of the psychoanalytical relationship must be understood, according to this view, in financial terms. Without the economics of the situation one cannot be expected to understand the dynamics of psychoanalysis. This view can be drawn from the radical indictment of Thomas Szasz in regards to the political, social, and economic influence on psychotherapy. Since Szasz does not believe there is such a thing as mental illness—all he allows for is some culturally bound justification of the prominent rhetorical and mystifying function of psychotherapy—he accuses psychotherapists and analysts of coercing confused people into a relationship from which only the therapist can gain (financially as well as psychologically), (Szasz 1974, 1987).

One modified or weaker version of the view regarding the reliance of psychology on economics claims that it is methodologically useful to take into account some of the economic principles that seem to guide the interaction between people when attempting to construct a psychological theory that accounts for the (rational) behavior of individuals in their society. In order to avoid the vagueness of such a version, it can be expressed in explicitly methodological terms, suggesting that economic methods of analysis should be (and have already been) employed in other fields, such as sociology and political science. This version focuses on the operational or instrumental importance and success of economic research methods (Cf., Radnitzky and Bernholz 1987).

Thinking about the methodological reduction of psychology to economics is already present in the debates of the previous century, when William Jevons, for instance, argued for the superiority of economics in its provision of mathematical models that allowed testing and immediate modifications (unlike psychological theories).[9] More recently, there have been numerous examples of trying to test psychological hypotheses using mathematically formulated versions of decision theory in order to measure beliefs concerning needs, desires, satisfaction, and happiness (Cf., Earl 1988, Arkes and Hammond 1986).

VI: DISCIPLINARY RELIANCE RECONSIDERED

The third view, that economics relies on psychology, seems historically and commonsensibly to describe with a different accuracy the relationship between these two disciplines. But, as mentioned above, the reliance can be understood ontologically or methodologically. In addition, the reliance may be understood in terms of succession or in hierarchical terms. One example in the history of economic thought that stands out in favor of this strong view is Philip Wicksteed's. His view addresses ontological reduction directly, and insists that economics, as known in his day, must be superseded.

Already in the beginning of the twentieth century, Wicksteed was claiming that the only way in which to understand the heavy dependence of economics on psychology is to view economics as nothing but "applied psychology." He explains that the terms used in political economy, like want, effort, desire, and satisfaction, are "each and all psychic phenomena." Psychological terms serve not merely as the building blocks of the theoretical superstructure of economics, but are simultaneously also the ultimate concerns of political economy, namely, the satisfaction of desires and happiness (Wicksteed 1933, 767).

In addition, Wicksteed claims that the four branches of economics—consumption, exchange, production, and distribution—all rely on the general psychological principle of diminishing returns of satisfaction. If there is any moral to be drawn from this description, according to Wicksteed, it is that economists should either devote their time to reexamine psychological principles and then become sociologists, or admit that their work is in the field of applied psychology and be aware of the absolute reliance of economics on psychology (Wicksteed 1933, 769). Either choice, of course, illustrates that economics can no longer claim any epistemological independence, and must become ipso facto subservient to psychology.

Wicksteed is not the sole example that can be provided for the third view concerning the relation between economics and psychology. Joseph A. Schumpeter, for example, claims that Menger and the Austrian School of Economics saw their work in the same terms described by Wicksteed, namely, as applied psychology (Schumpeter 1954, 1,057). Another noted historian of economic thought, Eric Roll, modified the strong view of the reliance implied by Wicksteed and claimed that Menger shifted away from a simple hedonistic interpretation of the principle of utility (Roll 1953, 386).

For economists and historians of economic thought there is a continued concern over the implications of admitting the reliance of economics on psychology. Would such reliance, in the sense of methodological reduction, necessarily lead one to think about an ontological reduction? Even though a distinction between these two sorts of reduction has been noted, there is still a lingering suspicion that the success of methodological reduction depends on the ability (even if never formally executed) of performing an ontological reduction. In other words, does a methodological commensurability entail a loss of autonomy?

This question is answered in the consideration of the fourth view concerning the relation of economics and psychology. According to this view, these two fields have much less in common than perceived in the previously discussed three views. Economics and psychology may be incommensurable in the sense that either field can be distinguished from the other on normative ground. For example, one can argue that economic theory is concerned with how people ought to behave, how they ought to follow certain rules (of rationality), and how they ought to respond (personally) to certain market forces. As such, the arguments on behalf of the competitive firm within a competitive marketplace can be seen against the background of the inefficiency of monopolistic tendencies. Characterizing the marketplace and the firms in these terms permits a conceptualization that favors certain modes of behavior, that encourages certain tendencies, while rejecting and warning against others.

In a similar fashion, one may argue that psychological theories, based on some metaphysical assumption concerning at least methodological but also ontological solipsism, are normative. The norms associated with psychology may be phrased in terms of what is perceived to be appropriate response to certain actions: how one should interact with others so as to maintain a certain level or friendliness (and avoid a certain level of hostility); or in terms of Kohlberg's developmental scale (Kohlberg 1981, 1984). In any of these instances, one can begin with a normative framework that is later supplemented with an experimental apparatus. But the empirical appeal is only post hoc, thereby distinguishing such an approach from others that maintain from the very start that their basis is empirical. Whether it is economics or psychology that is claimed to be a normative science (while the other is claimed to be empirical or natural or social), in either case it is possible to claim the incommensurability of the two fields. If both fields are normative (however defined), then there is no doubt that any notion of commensurability will become inoperable. Another way of expressing the incommensurability of both fields is in terms of the spectrum they each cover of the other field. For example, one can show that economics uses only a minimal set of psychological principles (and vice versa), so minimal in fact, that speaking of either methodological or ontological reduction makes no sense.

Looking at economics and psychology through distinct lenses retains all claims of autonomy either field may wish to maintain. That is, reduction between the fields is minimized so that issues of dependence become marginal. This issue is important because it is commonly understood that any sort of dependence, such as the ability to reduce a set of economic theories into a set of psychological principles, immediately robs economics of its autonomous status as a field of inquiry. A variant of such a view was explicitly expressed by Popper in his treatment of sociology (rather than economics). According to his view, there is a radical bifurcation between the concept and reality of reductionism of any sort and the concept and reality of independence of an area of research. That is, if a reduction is possible from one field into another, then the first field has no claim for any sort of independence.[10]

Must there be a necessary reduction from methodological to ontological reduction? Prior to either Wicksteed or Popper, two of the founders of modern economics responded in the negative. Both Smith and his teacher David Hume conceded that economics depends on psychology, even that we can reduce some economic ideas to psychological principles, but maintained that economics was and would remain an independent field of inquiry. The first three chapters of the first book of *The Wealth of Nations*, for example, are dominated by what we would term today a psychological analysis of the interaction between human beings in a free society, but this does not imply that it is not a treatise on economics.

The very notion that individuals are inclined to freely exchange their goods and even their labor power is rooted in psychological tendencies associated with self-interest and the desire to fulfill one's needs and wants, claim classical and neoclassical economists alike. But in no way does this sort of analysis force Smith or any of his followers to undermine or relinquish the independent status of economics. On the contrary, psychological principles are used as stepping stones from which to develop a whole new area of inquiry, as Lionel Robbins, for one, seems to agree. According to him, economists regard "the things which psychology studies as the data of their own deduction" (Robbins 1984, 86). And in no way does this or any other indebtedness to psychology deprive economics of its independence.[11]

VII: DISCIPLINARY INDEPENDENCE

There are two claims concerning the autonomous status of economics that can be distilled from the examination of the four views regarding the relationship between economics and psychology. First, that even if a reduction can be noticed between the two fields, it is only methodological and not ontological. That is to say, reduction of some sort does not entail the loss of independence for economics as a bona fide science. And second, that there may be no reason to find any reduction between the two fields, since they are coextensive fields of research, regardless of any passing references they may be making to each other in the course of their study. Both claims are related to one theme central to the history of economic thought: economics is an independent field of research, and, like any other such field, deserves expert and scientific status.

Understood in these terms, there is much at stake for economics, and perhaps for other sciences as well, in claiming independence and thereby defending their scientific credibility and legitimacy, for example in political terms (Sassower 1985, Ch. 5). It makes sense, in this light, for economics to parade the label of applied psychology, hoping to benefit from the scientific value granted to modern psychology. If psychology is indeed a bona fide science, and if economics relies heavily on the alleged scientific principles of psychology (if not on the details of its theoretical framework), then it is obviously true to claim that economics is a science that can profess expertise and independent status. So, it is important to establish the independence of economics, for with it comes the modern recognition of scientific worth and expert knowledge. Scientific worth can maintain the power and authority of economics, regardless of this or that disappointment with one or more predictions. That is, once scientific independence is granted to economics, there seems to be less, if any, need to continue and protect economics from challenges that it is neither independent nor scientific.

The alleged scientific credentials economists claim for their work can be used for the sake of instituting policies that they deem worthy for whatever political and ideological reasons. These reasons can remain hidden by their scientific appearance, as is the case with the contemporary Contestable Market Theory (Sassower 1988b). As such, the scientific legitimacy that psychology, or for that matter any other scientific field of inquiry, may confer on economics is so highly valued that questions of dependency may even be welcomed, not rejected.

But scientific legitimacy, in whatever form it appears, does not account for the particular position of economics as being at once natural and moral philosophy. This dichotomy precedes the kind of disciplinary squabbles that are documented here in the case of economics and psychology, and it is a dichotomy that informed intellectual activities right into the late nineteenth century. In what follows, I argue that one way to reconsider the entire discussion of disciplinary boundaries as expert formations is by aligning the notion of moral philosophy with that of natural philosophy.

VIII: POLITICAL ECONOMY AS NATURAL AND MORAL PHILOSOPHY

Beginning with the traditional dichotomy between natural and moral philosophy, it is possible to illustrate to what extent political economy can be classified in both areas simultaneously. One could extend this illustration and argue that any bona fide and independent area of research in the contemporary intellectual landscape falls into these two areas simultaneously as well. If this point can be illustrated and sustained, it can further the argument that disciplinary boundaries, though a necessary condition for the acquisition and dissemination of knowledge in contemporary culture, are artificial constructs that can be easily dispensed with and circumvented. If such a proposition is accepted, then our intellectual outlook and educational goals may look quite different in the future so that claims for expertise may appear in a different guise. That is, they could no longer be upheld with an appeal to scientific certitude, but instead would have to be examined critically from a pragmatic perspective.

Smith's works seem a useful device through which to examine the argument sketched above. Considered the founder of modern political economy, his works can at once illustrate two points. One, political economy is both natural and moral philosophy so that to talk about political economy in exclusive scientific terms fails to account for one of its important dimensions. And two, the shift after Smith's time from the label political economy to economics was a conscious attempt to set up the distinction between natural and moral philosophy, but without success. What is at issue is a craving for independent scientific and expert status under the assumption that such a status can be granted or denied regardless of specific moral aspects of one's research.

It is possible to argue that if one can demonstrate a continuity between Smith's moral and economic writings so that his works in some general sense are part of each other, then to argue that his work on political economy heralds the dawn of a new field of inquiry—a new science—is untenable. But this position, as argued above in connection with the relationship between economics and psychology, is not the purpose of this section. Instead, I attempt to show that no matter how research is narrowed or defined, it necessarily includes a moral dimension or has a normative dimension to it. The normative dimension can be described from a feminist perspective or from the perspective of literary criticism; it can be described critically in Marxian terms or apologetically in conservative terms. No matter how it is described, no matter how importantly the moral dimension figures in discussions about the field at hand, the very prospect that there is such a dimension that can be distilled from any field of research provides sufficient grounds to support the hypothesis here under investigation, namely, that all fields of inquiry are simultaneously involved in what has traditionally been defined as the dichotomy of natural and moral philosophy.

In reviewing Smith's two major works, the *Theory of Moral Sentiments* (1759) and *The Wealth of Nations* (1776), it is possible to support one of two views. The first view is that there is a continuity between these two works, and that in order to fully understand either one of them, one needs to consult and take into consideration the other. Since Smith wrote his work on political economy seven years after his moral work, most scholars claim that in order to understand Smith's economic theory, one must realize that his views on morality bear directly on his economic views. This view of the continuity in Smith's work may have its roots in the Hegelian notion of a world-history, a spiritual whole, or the all-encompassing approach to the study of humanity in its environment. Leaving aside more comprehensive views on the nature of the universe or the historical development of humanity, the continuity view finds its support from textual analysis.

The most crucial textual evidence used by those who hold the continuity view are the last words of Smith's *The Theory of Moral Sentiments*:

> I shall, in another discourse, endeavor to give an account of the general principles of law and government, and of the different revolutions they have undergone in the different ages and periods of society, not only in what concerns justice, but in what concerns police, revenue, and arms, and whatever else is the object of law. I shall not, therefore, at present enter into any further detail concerning the history of jurisprudence. (Smith 1976, 537)

This passage has been given as evidence to support the claim that Smith himself conceived of all his writings as parts of a whole, since he himself promises to complete the task he began in his treatise on moral sentiments at a later stage.

Glenn Morrow, for one, dismisses arguments about Smith's change of heart between his two major works (Smith's three years stay in France), and claims that though self-interest is more obvious a factor in *The Wealth of Nations*, it also appears among inferior virtues in *The Theory of Moral Sentiments*. Furthermore, it is the issue of regulative justice which would or would not effectively channel individual self-interests within a society. The principle of individual rights and ultimate liberty, according to Morrow, is the cornerstone for both works, and entails a single comprehensive worldview (Morrow 1928, 165–168). Morrow concludes, then, on the question of the continuity between Smith's two major works that:

> It might almost be said that the doctrine of sympathy is a necessary presupposition of the doctrine of the natural order expounded in the *Wealth of Nations* . . . Thus we arrive, by way of the *Moral Sentiments* at a deeper understanding of that individualism which is presented in the economic liberalism and laissez faire of the *Wealth of Nations*. (Morrow 1928, 178)

Morrow's argument in support of the continuity view is referred to by most scholars after him. T. D. Campbell, for example, supports the continuity view by making Smith's earlier work into a scientific work so as to eliminate any charge of radical difference between these two works (Campbell 1971, 18–19). Another supporter is D. A. Reisman, who explains that lines of demarcation between disciplines were less strict then from what can be found today, and that Smith followed his time in considering different aspects and disciplines as forming one science of humanity (Reisman 1976, 11), so that the Weberian notion of *Verstehen* becomes pertinent for such a view (Reisman 1976, 38–39). Andrew Skinner, in his support of the continuity view, says that the first work provides an account of the psychological assumptions upon which the second work's socio-economic analysis develops (Skinner 1979, 13). Elsewhere Skinner and Campbell argue that *The Wealth of Nations* portrays Smith's concerns for modern man who (due to an intensified division of labor) would become "as stupid and ignorant as it is possible for a human creature to become," and thus "adversely affect that capacity for moral judgment which had been considered in *The Theory of Moral Sentiments*" (Skinner and Campbell 1982, 168–169). They also explain that in both his works Smith deliberately discusses human conduct in terms of possible "means-ends" analyses applicable to both moral and economic actions (Skinner and Campbell 1982, ch. 9, 106–108).

The objections to the continuity view are lumped into what is called the "discontinuity" view. According to this view, there is a difference in approach and methodology between Smith's two great works, one that reveals Smith's intellectual development and the changes he was capable of making during his own lifetime. Moreover, supporting the discontinuity view and providing grounds for upholding it may serve as an instrument through which to appreciate the formation and emergence of political economy as a separate field of inquiry, where moral philosophy is separated from natural philosophy.

Going back to the last words—those that seem to suggest a self-reference from one work to another—in the first edition of *The Theory of Moral Sentiments*, one can note that they were only suggestive (they did not refer, even in later editions, to definite works he had completed), and that the topic least emphasized in his list of suggested topics for later consideration and elaboration was "revenue." Revenue is only mentioned in connection with "police," "arms," and the "law," and does not constitute a separate field of inquiry that is related to his moral studies. Jurisprudence, on the other hand, is directly connected by Smith's own words, and thus linked to his considerations of moral sentiments. Examining Smith's own words does not lend sufficient support to the continuity view.

One supporter of the discontinuity view, E. G. West, splits Smith's treatment of human sentiments into two domains or two levels: strong motives and higher motives. Accordingly, each of Smith's two major works deals with one domain or one level of human motives and sentiments. Discussing *The Theory of Moral Sentiments*, West says:

> True, he tells us that in his later book, *The Wealth of Nations*, that it is not from his benevolence that the butcher provides you with your dinner. But here, in effect, he tells us that it is not from self-interest that the butcher jumps into the river to save you from drowning. Self-interest lives side by side with benevolence. They are not incompatible; each has its part to play at the appropriate time; and exclusively to concentrate upon one dimension of life is seriously to distort the whole. (West 1976, 99)

George Stigler seems to be decidedly on the discontinuity side when he argues about the separation and independence of economics from psychology and uses as an example Smith's two great works. He says:

> A theory of behavior . . . could have come from psychology, but of course it did not. In fact Smith's professional work on psychology

(in the *Theory of Moral Sentiments*) bears scarcely any relationship to his economics, and this tradition of independence of economics from psychology has persisted despite continued efforts from Jennings (1855) to Herbert Simon and George Kalone to destroy it. (Stigler 1965, 28)

Stigler makes a strong claim for the discontinuity between Smith's psychological work, his moral philosophy, and his economic writings, his natural philosophy. Stigler's view, though directed more specifically at the question of the independence of economics, as discussed above, exemplifies a certain tendency among economists and scholars of the history of economic theory to note the shift in Smith's writings, which eventually led to the foundation of political economy as an independent field of inquiry, a science. Moreover, by illustrating a shift in Smith's work and his methodology, it is possible to maintain the separation between moral and natural philosophy.

However, it seems to me that no matter what textual credibility the discontinuity view holds, it must still account for textual examples where a continuity or overlap between moral and natural philosophy is apparent. Take, for instance, the question of slavery. Political philosophers, such as John Locke, have argued on moral grounds why one could not sell oneself into slavery, even voluntarily (Locke 1947, 132–133). In *The Wealth of Nations* Smith uses a non-moral or an economic approach to illustrate the benefits of abolishing slavery. Smith does not appeal in this work to any sentiments (be they higher or not), but argues from a strictly financial or economic perspective. Smith argues that it would benefit society not to have slaves because the cost of having slaves exceeds its return. Stated differently, Smith says that free people are more efficient and productive (because one need not waste time and money supervising their daily maintenance), and thus their freedom benefits society as a whole (Smith 1937, 81, 365–367, 554). But does the emphasis of approach make the whole discussion of slavery thereby a discussion within natural philosophy proper? Does not the very fact that Smith examines slavery necessarily move the discussion also into the domain of moral philosophy?

IX: NATURAL PHILOSOPHY AS MORAL PHILOSOPHY

One can recall the history of the past two centuries in the development of political economy or economics as a continuous struggle to come to terms with the difference between natural philosophy and moral philosophy. One can trace that struggle in terms of the multiplicity of definitions given to the terms political economy and economics. The differences in definitions are testimonies to the conflicts of economists who simultaneously wish to be perceived as "scientists" and at the same time admit that their studies are committed to a certain morality or can support a certain view of morality.

One is tempted to deal with Marx on the question of the boundaries of political economy separately from "other" classical political economists of his day. Rather than sandwich his views between those of the classical and the neoclassical schools, it seems usually more appropriate to distinguish him from other economists because of his philosophical orientation and the dramatic changes he brought to light for anyone wishing to study the relation between economic conditions and sociopolitical institutions. Marx, on this view, is not merely another economist nor simply a critic of economic theory; instead, he is considered the founder of a school so different from the genealogy of economic thought that he deserves to be on his own, alone.

But is Marx's view on the natural and moral dimension of political economy different from his predecessors' and followers'? To begin with, the answer may be yes, since the Marxian conception of political economy is at once humanistic, that is, puts humans at the center of the analysis and also scientific in the sense of examining the variables provided by classical economists and critically analyzing them. In the *1844 Manuscripts* Marx says that the commodification of all needs has turned the economy or the marketplace from a place where individuals satisfy their needs into a place where alienated individuals seem to exchange their wares (labor power) in a manner that can never fully satisfy them (Marx 1964, 168).

Where does the economist fit in this picture? What role does the economist as an observer play? In one respect, the economist is a bourgeois agent, a hired-gun who produces rationalizations and justifications for the classical model without challenging its very theoretical foundations. Since Marx's economist only pretends not to speak the language of moral philosophy but ends up moralizing with every step of the so-called scientific analysis, political economy itself is understood as moral philosophy. In Marx's words: "Thus, despite its worldly and pleasure-seeking appearance, it is a truly moral science, and the most moral of all sciences." (Marx 1964, 171)

Though Marx argues that political economy is moral philosophy, his critique means to say that political economy of the classical school is immoral philosophy since its authors "advocate luxury and condemn saving" (Marx 1964, 172). But this, one may argue, is an all too simple an interpretation of political economy. To call it moral philosophy does not entail that its principles and prescription be moral in a specific Marxian sense; it may suffice to say, as discussed above, that it deals with or examines moral issues while analyzing the workings of the marketplace. Marx makes it seem that political economy is either moral or immoral, instead of acknowledging that it is a moral philosophy proper and that specific disagreements about principles, motives, and procedures may continue to be challenged no matter who describes the economy or prescribes its changes.

At this textual juncture, Marx seems to be falling into the same theoretical categories and bifurcations that informed Smith and his contemporaries and led them into an ambivalent position regarding the ability to distinguish between the science of political economy and its morality. In Marx's words:

> Everything which you own must be made venal, i.e. useful. Suppose I ask the economist: am I acting in accordance with economic laws if I earn money by the sale of my body, by prostituting it to another person's lust (in France, the factory workers call the prostitution of their wives and daughters the nth hour of work, which is literally true); or if I sell my friends to the Moroccans (and the direct sale of men occurs in all civilized countries in the form of the trade in conscripts)? He will reply: you are not acting contrary to my laws, but you must take into account what Cousin Morality and Cousin Religion have to say. My *economic* morality and religion have no objection to make, but . . . But then whom should we believe, the economist or the moralist? The morality of political economy is *gain*, work, thrift and sobriety—yet political economy promises to satisfy my needs. The political economy of morality is the riches of a good conscience, of virtue, etc., but how can I be virtuous if I am not alive and how can I have a good conscience if I am not aware of anything? The nature of alienation implies that each sphere applies a different and contradictory norm, that morality does not apply the same norm as political economy, etc., because each of them is a particular alienation of man; [XVII] each is concentrated upon a specific area of alienated activity and is itself alienated from the other. (Marx 1964, 173)

The introduction of "Cousin Morality" and "Cousin Religion" into the description and critique of classical political economy is a clear indication, as Marx says later, that there are different spheres of human activity that deal with different issues, so much so that they are "alienated" from each other. This way of speaking about political economy and morality, as relatives but not so close so as to be siblings, gives credence to the reading of Smith's two major works as somehow remotely connected, but not really one continuous work.

If so far it seems that Marx's words indicate the sort of ambivalence evidenced in the works of classical political economists, his own critique of one of Ricardo's critics sets his own view in a clear manner:

> Thus M. Michel Chevalier reproaches Ricardo with leaving morals out of account. But Ricardo lets political economy speak its own lan-

guage; he is not to blame if this language is not that of morals. M. Chevalier ignores morals, but he really and necessarily ignores morals when he is concerned with political economy; for the bearing of political economy upon morals is either arbitrary and accidental and thus lacking any scientific basis or character, is a mere *sham*, or else it is *essential* and can then only be a relation between economic laws and morals. If there is no such relation can Ricardo be held responsible? Moreover, the antithesis between morals and political economy is itself only *apparent*; there is an antithesis and equally no antithesis. Political economy expresses, *in its own fashion*, the moral laws. (Marx 1964, 173–174)

Even though Marx is commonly allocated a separate intellectual space in regards to his theory of political economy, especially in terms of exploitation and alienation, his overall view of political economy is just as confused as that of Smith. Moreover, when pushed on the question of identifying political economy as either a natural or a moral philosophy, he seems to perpetuate the myth of the scientific foundations and methods used by economists. Economists, from this perspective, are not moralists. But can this posture endure further scrutiny?

As the illustration of the case of Malthus in chapter 2 shows, it is difficult to sustain this view of the separation between moral and natural philosophy for the case of political economy and perhaps for other fields of inquiry as well. One need not refer back to the history of the terms economics and political economy in order to fully appreciate the historico-linguistic transformation that reflected a change in attitude toward the activities of political economists (e.g., Sassower 1985, Appendix I). And one need not search for a multiple of examples that demonstrate to what extent so-called natural philosophy turns out to be in fact moral philosophy as well.

When an economic theory, like Malthus', generates predictions, they are crucial in formulating policies which have immediate effects, regardless of the precision and eventual success or failure of these predictions. The original theoretical framework that gave rise to these predictions may be forgotten altogether, but the results that emanated from this same framework will have an impact for some time. That is, whether the theory is in the domain of political economy or sociology, physics, or psychology, the very modeling that generates the theory has an effect regardless of potential objections or outright rejections. What turns natural philosophy into moral philosophy is not only the moral presupposition or even predispositions that enter into a particular formulation but also the policy impact that flows from the specific study and one that has a moral—social, political, and economic—impact on society.

Whether or not Smith as well as Marx seem ambiguous about the lines of demarcation or connection between moral philosophy and political economy, Malthus' case dispels their ambiguity concerning the separation of moral concerns and convictions from an allegedly purely scientific study. But if the separation cannot be sustained, what does it mean to say that the boundaries between or among disciplines are blurred? If there is no difference, say, between psychology and economics, are they one and the same? If there is no difference between natural and moral philosophy, does it necessarily mean that every scientific prediction has moral overtones?

These questions can no longer be dismissed offhand, but require a close scrutiny by society, so that alleged scientific recommendations by so-called experts would be approached and acted upon on more than one level of response. That is, instead of accepting scientific results as if they were divorced from any moral consideration, the presumption must be the opposite: unless one can demonstrate that there are no moral considerations relevant to a particular case at hand, moral questions should be raised to the scientific community, the community of scientific and technological experts, in some of the forms examined in the next chapter.

CHAPTER 5

Politicizing Expertise

I: INTRODUCTION

As seen so far, expertise can be understood differently, depending on specific contexts. For example, the expertise discussed in chapter 1 was restricted to scientists who belonged to the BAAS. Within their organization, experts listened to each other and only occasionally involved the public in their deliberations and decisions. Yet, as we recall, the BAAS was dedicated to the proliferation of the results of scientific research in public forums, and as such illustrates one dimension of the interrelation between experts and the public.

Chapters 2 and 3, in their respective ways, tried to show the historical shift from oracles to experts as a shift only in degrees of psychological desire to listen to others and accept their pronouncements. Whether the talk is of oracles or sophists in earlier times or of experts or scientists in contemporary culture, the epistemological stock we put in the words of others reflects our own psychological anxieties. But before I move on to reexamine the linkage between epistemology and psychology, it may help to review some standard arguments about the relationship that should exist between experts and society, between the scientific or technoscientific community and the public.

In order to survey the views on the social and political role of experts in our midst, we should recall the discussion of chapter 4, where disciplinary boundaries were blurred, and where the privileged status of the sciences is criticized, whether applied to political economy directly, to the social sciences in general, or to all the sciences indirectly. From this context I borrow an elastic sense of who to include in the group of experts, for they need not be natural scientists or social scientists exclusively. Experts include physicians and lawyers, electricians and musicians, dancers and nuclear physicists, philosophers and sophists. One may object that there are great differences between the theoretical and the practical matrices within which each one of these professionals works. That may be true to some extent, but that will not change the general observations made in regards to the role of experts or specialists in our midst, the performative roles they play and the reception of their performances.

I also believe that by now expertise as a privileged, divine-like attribute, has been contextualized and understood pragmatically in this book. In this light, then, it is possible for the public to assess the recommendations of experts and choose what to make of them. The public is itself a broad term that must be used more cautiously in the pages that follow. At this point I mean the public at large, educated or not, participating in policy issues or not. As will be seen later, I will have to qualify the term public at times to include only the majority of the public commonly perceived in democratic societies, democratic in the broadest sense of a twentieth-century representative governmental order based on a constitution and/or bill of rights.

One narrative about the social role of experts that has become standard in the literature stipulates the following two extreme positions. On the one hand, experts are in a superior political and social position so that their advice and decisions dominate public policies. On the other hand, experts may be put in such an inferior position that their advice is ignored regardless of its merits. Either position can miss a useful tool with which to make public policies. In democratic institutions, expert knowledge can be in the service of the public for endorsement or criticism, depending on particular circumstances. A third view can be constructed so that it enjoys the advantages of these two views without suffering their weaknesses. I take this third view to be conducive for the increase of public participation in establishing policies. I also believe that in addition to its merits in political (increased participatory democracy) and moral (increased individual expression of rights and duties) terms, there are psychological merits to this view. For example, even when mistakes are made, public resentment, frustration, and anger will be minimal because the mistakes were not made by experts but by the public itself. That is, one can argue that an individual is more self-forgiving than forgiving others who, so to speak, should have known better.

This way of perceiving the interaction between experts and the public (or its majority that participates through voting) differs from the Habermasian notion of expert "compromise," where different elite groups negotiate their differences and reach a consensus in some procedure of "ideal speech acts" (Habermas 1975). Moreover, suggesting public debates that rely on criteria other than those derived from a Kantian notion of rationality serves here as a critique of the Habermasian or, for that matter, any other elitist orientation. Yes, I conceive of expert activity and advice that are detached from public debates and the media—whether undertaken by the American Medical Association or a group of nuclear scientists lodged in Los Alamos, New Mexico—to be elitist, elitist in the sense of privileging their procedures and posture vis-à-vis the culture in which they take place.

This chapter is about the social and political role of experts, scientists, and technicians in contemporary society; in this sense it is political in its orientation. But, as becomes apparent, the criticism of various models of relations (between experts and the public) is itself political and moral and therefore cannot simply be classified as philosophical. Just as disciplinary boundaries have become blurred, just as the distinction between natural and moral philosophy no longer holds sway in the contemporary context, so I will show how any discussion of the social role of experts (so common in the literature) should deal with moral and psychological issues as well. Once cast is this broader mode of examination, there will be room for asking questions about responsibility and duty in personal and not only in broad political or philosophical terms.

II: THE POLITICS OF SCIENCE

It is possible to focus on the social and political role of scientists (including physicians and lawyers) as intellectual leaders and experts within their culture in order to articulate a set of standards or rules by which democratic societies should interact with experts. It is also possible to acknowledge the importance of procedural rules by which to guide expert involvement in public policy and proceed to examine some of the psychological issues that influence and are influenced by delegating decision-making authority to experts. In what follows, I begin with the former possibility in order to set the stage for talking about the latter.

Some of what follows appears as an exercise in classification, wherein different views or positions are juxtaposed against each other as if there is a clear dichotomy between them. As explained in chapter 4, such an exercise is a heuristic means that familiarizes us with the literature on the subject matter in order to do something different with it. That is, I enter the game/discourse of "the cultural role of experts" or "the politics of science" so that my move to a different game/discourse, say, "the psychological aspects of expert authority" will not overlook important issues raised in the previous game/discourse. Assuming that all narratives and games are interconnected in a labyrinth (Ormiston and Sassower 1989), it seems useful to proceed from one game/discourse to another, borrowing liberally from whatever seems useful.

Whatever label is given to the game played out in the following pages, it is a game wherein experts and the public—as two artificially distinguished groups of people—interact in accordance with a set of rules they help set up themselves. Some of these rules were set already during the Enlightenment Age in a way that was meant to bring closer the two groups in a democratized society. In 1795, Antoine-Nicolas de Condorcet asked the following rhetorical question: "Has not printing freed the education of the people from all political and religious shackles?" (Condorcet 1979, 102) For an eighteenth-century "enlightened" mind, the answer was quite obviously, yes. The technological innovations of the printing press in the late fifteenth century enabled "the people," as Condorcet calls them, to venture into the mysterious and until then cloistered world of the intellectuals, the clergy, and the aristocrats. If there was any hope for the progress of the human mind, he continues, it was through the proliferation of knowledge and the subordination of authority to reason.

From Condorcet's perspective, then, one can stipulate that the activities one associates with science and technology are politically potent, whether one recognizes them as such or not. If science and technology are always political, at least in the sense of having the potential to free one from the shackles of political and religious authority, what is the political "game" of science and technology? Some two hundred years after Condorcet, one finds echoes of his vision of the rules of this game—accompanied with his populist sentiment concerning the political benefits of science and technology (but not in terms of the perfectibility of human nature and its intellectual capacities)—in both the so-called political right and left. Oddly enough, the two extremes of the political spectrum (as commonly defined in the western, popular press) find common ground in their attitudes toward the relationship that ought to exist between an elite of scientific and technological experts and the community of people among whom they live. Though the sentiment is shared—that experts are public servants who should be scrutinized continuously by the public through its representatives—its rationale or justification is different.

For the so-called political right, every individual has the same rights and obligations as any other, and therefore no individual, no matter how expert, should be privileged by comparison to another. No elites can be justified from the standpoint of radical individualism or even libertarianism. At the same time, the so-called political left finds it unacceptable to allow any elite to be sanctioned by any political body, for it may undermine the ultimate authority of the people and thereby hamper the power of the public to decide for itself whatever is in its best interest. The goals of a classless society, a society in which every individual contributes to the welfare of all others while enjoying the collective fruits produced by all other individuals, do not justify or legitimate an elite of experts not subordinate and accountable to the rest of society.

Instead of tracing the narratives of these two traditions concerning their attitudes toward the control of experts, I assume that both traditions cast a suspicious and critical eye toward such elitist institutions and individuals (e.g., Dhombres 1988 and Pockley 1988). Surveys show, however, that the public in the U.S. during the period of 1947–1982 has consistently found scientists and the scientific community in general to be only second (to physicians and the medical profession) in the ranking of respectability, esteem, and confidence (Khan 1988). The suspicion of, say, anything elitist does not necessarily mean that the public distrusts experts or would like them to disappear. There is, then, a possible accommodation between experts and the public, one that avoids the confrontational attitude one would assume from what was mentioned earlier about the so-called political right and left.

The power game, if one wants to call it by this name, between experts and the public need not be perceived as being confrontational nor one where the public is by definition at a disadvantage. As Machiavelli reminds us:

> Contrary to the general opinion, then, which maintains that the people, when they govern, are inconsistent, unstable, and ungrateful... it would almost seem as if the people had some occult virtue, which enables them to foresee the good and the evil. As to the people's capacity of judging of things, it is exceedingly rare that, when they hear two orators of equal talents advocate different measures, they do not decide in favor of the best of the two; which proves their ability to discern the truth of what they hear (Machiavelli 1977, 113–114).

Machiavelli's words credit the public with an ability to make judgments regardless of any suspicion or skepticism. Within this context, then, I propose to clarify more specifically how democratic institutions and structures set additional rules for the game of experts examined here.

III: LEADERSHIP AND DEMOCRACY

For present purposes, I adopt Robert Dahl's version of what criteria would satisfy an ideal democratic process. To begin with, an ideal democracy is not understood in terms of a definite constitution or a set of laws, but rather as a "process" that changes over time, but which must adhere to certain guidelines. According to Dahl, there are five criteria that must be satisfied in a democratic process: (1) equality in voting, (2) effective participation, (3) enlightened understanding, (4) final control of the agenda in the hands of the body of citizens, and (5) inclusion of all adults within the political arena (Dahl 1982, 6).

In what follows, I will consider Dahl's second criterion as central to the others he presents, for in it one can determine to what extent the others are fulfilled. For example, without what Dahl calls "enlightened understanding" one may wonder to what extent, if at all, there is an "effective" participation, as opposed to a participation that can be overlooked altogether. It goes without saying that one cannot reduce the five criteria into one, nor that it is possible to do away with any of them. For instance, if there is no equality of voting in effect, one cannot expect that there will be an effective participation, since a great number of citizens will not be participating at all in the decision-making process. Finally, one could argue that if the final control of the political agenda is with citizens, it is possible to expect effective participation. However, such an argument does not necessarily hold when the definition of effectiveness emphasizes, to use Dahl's term, an "enlightened understanding", while the notion of control over the agenda may not be enlightened at all.

In a manner similar to Dahl's, Popper insists on an institutional framework within which political changes ought to take place, where reforms and enlightened understanding in Dahl's sense constitute what Popper calls the use of reason and "self-criticism" (Popper 1971, I, 130). For Popper, "only democracy provides an institutional framework that permits reform without violence, and so the use of reason in political matters" (Popper 1971, I, 4). Thinking of democracy in discursive terms, Popper claims that if the discourse blocks dissent and criticism, then it is perceived as and is defined in terms of tyranny; if the discourse encourages dissent and criticism, allows for reforms and changes, then it is considered democratic (Popper 1971, II, 151).

Evaluating democratic institutions, then, requires a consideration of the tools of the trade, the techniques that are operable—linguistic and other. Here one can perceive a connection between the epistemological debates in philosophy of science and technology and the debates over the democratization of these institutions and their debates (in too often jargonized and exclusive manner). For example, sociologists of science have raised questions concerning the efficiency of the democratic model of representative government within the context of the scientific community. These kinds of questions have helped to articulate a more specific sense of a scientific community or a community of experts instead of continuing to talk in broad terms about experts (e.g., on democratizing the medical community see Agassi 1990).

Thomas Kuhn, for one, agrees with Michael Polanyi that when one speaks of science, one is in fact speaking of a scientific community. When speaking of scientific heroes, such as Newton or Darwin, who were presumed to produce their works of genius in an intellectual vacuum, it is understood that scientists acquire a special cultural status because they were leaders—in the sense of setting an agenda—of whole communities. Polanyi talks, for instance, of the scientific community requiring its members to subscribe to the rules of their game "by an act of devotion"; he speaks of the "tradition of science" and of "allegiance" (Polanyi 1964, 54). Kuhn continues this line of thought, and describes the "initiation" into the scientific community and the necessary "insulation" from the rest of society (Kuhn 1970, 164–165). If this is an accurate description of the structure of the scientific community, it is the leadership that requires study and not only this or that specific text in which a new theory or a new principle is articulated.

Assuming that scientific and technological communities have a leadership, as Polanyi and Kuhn argue approvingly, I will discuss the aforementioned two views on the relation between experts and the public in terms of their leaderships (assuming, along democratic rules of behavior, that they are representative of their group).[1] Emphasizing the posture of leaderships allows me to focus on the power relations between leaders and their own community as well as their relations with the public at large. In doing so, I disagree with the view presented by Kuhn that "One of the strongest, if still unwritten, rules of scientific life is the prohibition of appeals to heads of states or to the populace at large in matters scientific" (Kuhn 1970, 168).

IV: TWO OPPOSING VIEWS OF EXPERTS AND THEIR PUBLIC

If any balance is to be struck between the need for specialization and its usefulness in daily activities and the need to curb the dangers involved in the pronouncements of experts/specialists in matters of public policy, then it may be helpful to delineate the extreme views regarding the matter. At one extreme there are those who argue that specialization is not only needed, but must be encouraged as the only means by which to accomplish any social and economic progress. One vocal proponent of this position is George Stigler.

Stigler concedes that "defense of specialism in academic life ranks just above defense of racial prejudice" (Stigler 1984, 10). Yet he contends that research specialization is the most efficient way to expend limited (by definition, for him) intellectual and technical resources for the benefit of society as a whole.[2] In his argument, Stigler follows Smith's model of the division of labor for economic production, extending it into the intellectual sphere: "specialism is the royal road to efficiency in intellectual as in economic life" (Stigler

1984, 12). Stigler continues to reject all possible objections to his glorification of the importance and contribution of specialists. He argues that when problems that affect the public require the input of specialists from a variety of fields, there should be no problem integrating their insights (instead of destroying their separate areas of specialized research). There is also no danger, according to his view, that specialization will result in narrow-mindedness and duplication of efforts, because he believes in the individuality of specialists and their diverse, creative minds. This mode of intellectual production would inform the expert leadership and would have it represent the ideas of individual experts and not concentrate power in the hands of few individuals. What Stigler prescribes for the expert community's internal workings—a free marketplace-like exchange of ideas—spills into this community's relation with the public.

Stigler's view represents one extreme of a continuum of views regarding the preferred mode of interaction between the scientific leadership and the public. According to this view, specialists should be secured a special position in the political fabric of society, since they are important public benefactors. Without them modern society would remain undereducated, attempting to retain a level of general knowledge wholly inappropriate for the technological demands it faces. Specialists, then, should be heralded as the heroes of modern society, and their status of leadership with attendant power should not be challenged. One way of thinking about this view in political terms, even democratic ones in particular, is the notion of the rule of elites in Habermas' sense.

Noticing that "the political consequences of the authority enjoyed by the scientific system in developed societies is ambivalent" (Habermas 1975, 84), Habermas concedes that "democracy no longer has the goal of rationalizing authority through the participation of citizens in discursive processes of will-formation" (Habermas 1975, 123). Here he echoes the notions of democracy used above in Dahl's and Popper's texts, but which go along with Max Weber as well, at least in the sense of enlightened understanding, self-criticism, and rational discourse. For Habermas, the ideal speech situation includes communication procedures that are supposed to guarantee some sort of consensus, some presumption as to the common ground or shared values and the belief in the importance of reason and rationality (Habermas 1975, 105). But what if such an ideal cannot be realized? What if such an ideal does not induce all citizens to participate in the communication process with experts, and thus fails to fulfill one of the criteria set by Dahl?

In such a situation, according to Habermas, and given the authority and power of experts (scientists, for him) in developed societies, what will result is "possible *compromises* between ruling elites" (Habermas 1975, 123). From this perspective, then, regardless of Habermas' objection or endorsement of this possible scenario, one can conclude with Stigler that the compromises achieved by ruling elites will be better than those reached by a single elite, scientific or political, or by the public. One may object that there is a great deal of difference between a decision reached by an elite of experts (in whatever field) that is not democratically elected and the decision reached by democratically elected representatives. But as this position illustrates, the compromise itself is perceived as a democratic procedure, and thus can be justified as the best possible situation of the interaction between scientific elites or a scientific leadership and all others (elected or not).

At the other extreme of the continuum of views concerning the relations between expert leaders and public leaders are those who argue that experts/specialists are public enemies whose activities should be monitored and even curtailed whenever necessary. One proponent of this view is Paul Feyerabend who argues that experts/specialists pose a threat to democracy. Just as Stigler uses Smith's classical notion of the division of labor, so does Feyerabend use a classical liberal notion of individual liberty as it was developed by John S. Mill. If modern liberal society has progressed at all, it has done so by becoming the provisional bastion of democracy. Democratic society allows leadership, but for this leadership to exert any power it requires the consent of at least a majority. If specialists constitute only a minority, then they ought to be subservient to the rule of the majority of laypeople. Speaking of the relationship between experts and the public, the salient issue is majoritarian democracy, namely, that any decision is executed only if it has the consent of the majority. In this sense, then, expert suggestions must be left open to appropriate or mistaken choices of the majority of the public or its representatives (Feyerabend 1978, 86–87 and Agassi 1985, 57).

But is it not true that specialists have specialized knowledge whose authority is warranted by its approximation to the truth? Not at all, according to Feyerabend, who follows the Popperian approach as to the tentative status of scientific claims and argues that scientific knowledge is no different from any other knowledge (for example, religious knowledge) in its relationship to ideology, may it be that of the church or that of rationality. Preferring the one to the other may or may not be reasonable; but claiming that science is free of ideology is untrue (Feyerabend 1978, 88–91). Besides, scientific claims may turn out to be just as false as other, nonscientific claims. Just because knowledge claims are claimed to be scientific should not cloud our minds as to their putative or tentative status vis-à-vis what they consider to be the Truth.

Given these reasons, Feyerabend invites scientists and nonscientists alike to join the debates that may seem to be exclusively in the domain of scientific expertise, no matter in what particular specialty. If there is any message in his declarations, it is that we should banish the distinguished status we have given to specialists or scientific leaders, and retain their advice as yet another piece of information necessary for our decision-making processes.

One can note here that, as Allan Mazur argues, "the political, nonscientific context of the [scientific] dispute—e.g., McCarthyism or environmentalism—might be equally important in determining the outcome" (Mazur 1973, 245). Besides, experts are called upon to make "judgements for which there are no formalised guides and it is here that experts frequently disagree" (Mazur 1973, 251). Mazur concludes by saying that the "value of technical expertise" is questionable, especially for policymakers (Mazur 1973, 261). This conclusion supports Feyerabend's position when it is viewed as a democratic position rather than a position that wishes to eliminate or radically curtail the power of experts: society, or "duly elected committees of laymen" as Feyerabend calls them, must be the final arbiters as to the value of expert advice (Feyerabend 1978, 96).

So, which view should we adopt, the one represented by Stigler or the one represented by Feyerabend? Should society—through its political leadership—become so skeptical and suspicious of scientific leaderships that it should diminish the force of their recommendations? Or, should the public—in a majoritarian democratic fashion—follow scientific leaderships and grant them unrestricted freedom to pursue their own agenda? The answers to these questions may depend to a great extent on the range of available relevant choices, adopting a pragmatic approach. For instance, if the concern is with a certain piece of data that can be tested by a series of chemical reactions that are experimented with in a laboratory, then society may relegate the authority of finding that particular piece of data to chemists. But if the concern is with social questions that include so many variables for which no single model can fully account, then society may wish to view experts and specialists not as leaders at all, but as civil servants who produce relevant pieces of data.

V: A COMPROMISE WITH EXPERTS

One proponent of a compromise view is Harold Laski who says "But it is one thing to urge the need for expert consultation at every stage of making policy; it is another thing, and a very different thing, to insist that experts' judgment must be final" (Laski 1931, 4). The expert, then, can become an adviser whose views are solicited because they are valuable for society's purposes. But this solicitation should not turn into submission. The final decision remains, as Feyerabend argues, with the people, or as Laski calls them in quite a derogatory and sexist way, "plain men."

There is a danger that experts will become so removed from plain people that the concern of these people may no longer be at the heart of their advice. Besides, "plain" people have one attribute that is important for coming to agreement on social policies as noted already by Machiavelli, their common sense. But expertise, according to Laski, often overlooks the simplicity and beauty of common sense, and thereby violates even the most basic avenues of reasoning (Laski 1931, 4–7). An echo of Laski's concern with the removal of experts from the rest of the population is also found in Arnold Pacey's treatment of the culture of technology. There he illustrates the extent to which modern society has allowed the separation between "expert sphere" and "user sphere" (Pacey 1983, Ch. 3), a separation that parallels to some extent C. P. Snow's concern with the "two cultures" (Snow 1986). This presumed separation, of course, defines the rules of the game used in the interaction between experts and the public, where issues of translation from one linguistic apparatus to another is of great importance.

According to Laski, the specialist "is an invaluable servant and an impossible master" (Laski 1931, 10). Why are experts unfit to rule? Why are specialists not political leaders in the sense defined above? Laski claims that they are trained to become narrow-minded and concerned only with their own research, with their own data. What they lack is the ability to coordinate their specialized knowledge (as envisioned by Stigler) with the specialized knowledge of others (that of their colleagues or that of political leaderships). They may do so, but only for the sake of advancing their own specialized area of research, without concern for the benefit to society as a whole (Laski 1931, 10–11). That is, they do not endorse the compromises of ruling elites because they do not grant equal weight to the recommendations of other elites or special interest groups. The Habermasian ideal of a compromise becomes an exercise of incommensurable language games, because of the refusal to talk and listen to each other (or translate from one language to another). Lastly, Laski shows a concern for the lack of moral consideration in the advice of expert leaderships. For him, moral considerations are part and parcel of any social policy and are open to public debate, as was discussed at the end of chapter 4. When expert advice is not embedded in a system of values or does not account for possible ethical implications that accompany it, then the advice is useless, even dangerous (Laski 1931, 12–13).

Laski's concern with the moral fabric of society is also echoed in the writing of Langdon Winner who is concerned with the political aspects of our technological age. Winner is aware of the possible disagreement and division among experts or within the so-called expert leaderships in relation to a specific scientific or technological question.[3] This situation leads him to declare that "the norms that regulate the acceptance or rejection of the findings of scientific research become, in effect, moral norms governing judgments about harm and responsibility" (Winner 1986, 143). Because these are moral norms and not only scientific norms, they require the participation of the public and do not permit the delegation of authority to a leadership for the purpose of making policy decisions.

Winner would therefore agree with Laski's lament at the conclusion of his pamphlet: "To strike a balance between necessary respect and sceptical attack is a difficult task" (Laski 1931, 14). The difference between experts and the public is one that requires a strong sense of tolerance to overcome mutual impatience (Cf., Polanyi 1964, 67–68). Mutual patience and respect may allow the public— through the deliberations of its leadership or through public forums and referendum—to tolerate expert leaderships, even respect them and solicit their advice, but still maintain a critical distance between expert advice and public policy that draws from that very advice (Agassi 1985, 72–75).

One may object and argue that laypeople are never justified in rejecting the advice of experts. That is, public ignorance is such that if expert advice were rejected by the public just because it is expert advice, it would be a whimsical rejection, not based on good reasons. Does the public not depend on experts to phrase the very issues about which decisions are to be made, posit possible alternatives for action, and predict the consequences associated with every possible choice? So, though the public is invited to participate in the debate with experts—in direct open meetings or through the negotiations of leaderships—it is quite unreasonable to expect that the majority of the public should have the final say in matters that require some expert background knowledge.

Besides, even if one were to acknowledge that there is some public discontent with experts, their role, status, and power, this does not mean that experts can be easily replaced with nonexperts, or that scientific and technological research can be accomplished without experts. If there is some skepticism by the public toward expertise, it is more of an anti-intellectual sentiment in Richard Hofstadter's sense (Hofstadter 1962) and not necessarily an anti-professional sentiment of the kind described by Burton Bledstein (Bledstein 1978). Put differently, it is a mistake to confuse public outrage that reflects ardent individualistic sentiments of the entrepreneurial sort (suspicious of any kind of leadership) with a philosophical skepticism that has been linked in this book with Lyotard's and Popper's legacies.

Bertrand Russell who would endorse Laski's compromise view agrees that "it is necessary to train a large number of rather narrow specialists" (Russell 1950, 21). But Russell cautions against the acceptance of any scientific claims of certainty because they may never be substantiated (at least in the Popperian sense, but, of course, also in the Lyotardian sense). Instead of putting his faith (as Laski recommends) in the common sense of the public, Russell emphasizes the training of the scientific community in philosophy.

According to Russell, "it is philosophy that shows the right attitude, by making clear at once the scope and the limitations of scientific knowledge" (Russell 1950, 25). Focusing on scientists as experts, Russell contrasts the "right" attitude of philosophy with the inappropriate attitudes of those who either "pooh-pooh" science or think that science is "everything." These "other" attitudes may lead back to superstitious beliefs (if science is ignored altogether) or to complacency (if science is regarded as delivering the "final word"). Russell does not wish to do away with specialists, only to encourage them to broaden their horizons so that the concerns of society at large may help them in their own narrow pursuits (Russell 1950, 32–33). A similar sentiment is offered by Niels Bohr, who hopes that "in spite of the ever increasing specialization in science as well as in technology, [our generation] has a growing feeling of the mutual dependency of all human activities" (Bohr 1955, I, 28). Are philosophers excluded from the charge of being experts and therefore capable of mediating between the leaderships of experts and the public? Chapter 6 tries to address this question.

But, will a dose of "liberal" education eliminate the potential hazards associated with the rule of experts? Is there a direct link between knowledge (scientific or liberal) and virtue, between what Lyotard calls descriptions and prescriptions, between natural and moral philosophy? And, of course, would the education of scientists to be sensitive to public concerns not create a situation more devastating in terms of the concentration of power than was ever envisioned before? That is, scientists would be in a position to determine in a paternalistic fashion what is good for society as a whole without needing to consult society or its representatives at all, having the moral training they deem proper for their deliberations. Would it not be preferable, even if quite untenable, to insist on the education of the public at large so that it would be in a better, more "enlightened" (in Dahl's sense) position to evaluate the advice of specialists?

The response to Laski's challenge, Russell's or Bohr's, may be dismissed as elitist: in a Habermasian fashion, they trust specialists to think about the welfare of society so that science would be at the service of society. But, are such recommendations trustworthy? Are they not self-serving, at least in the sense of securing the independence of scientists from overt social and political constraints?[4] The compromise view that delineates the relations between experts and the public would have to respond to these questions by giving added power to the public, under the rules of democracy, in figuring out what should be executed as public policy. I would add that this view should circumscribe its rules of action in a pragmatic, contextual manner similar to the one advocated by Lyotard. In other words, sometimes there will be the advice of expert leaderships that will convince political leaderships, for example, on the safety of nuclear power plants. But such an agreement between these leaderships does not preclude the possibility that a (public or scientific) minority would oppose the majority. Democratic procedures allow the majority to prevail, but they also allow for minorities to voice their opinion and fight for the reconsideration of the decisions agreed upon before so that the majority may change its mind or a different majority will emerge.

VI: PERSONAL PUBLIC INVOLVEMENT

The survey just concluded deals in general terms with the question of the social role of experts in our midst, and does not account for the reaction and behavior of individual citizens that find themselves either in the majority or the minority of a democratically structured society. In order to connect certain themes already introduced in previous chapters as well as themes that will be presented in the next chapter, I want to end this chapter with a focus on the personal dimension (as opposed to public posture) of the encounters we have with experts.

My concern is to encourage personal involvement whenever possible, given the usual constraints one has in terms of time and accessibility to materials and specialized data. Instead of reading about the possible relations between expert leaderships and the political leaderships that represent us and expecting the relationship to be decided by those two sets of leaderships alone, I would like to see increased individual probing into the questions and issues posed above. That is, I would like to see political notions such as duty, responsibility, and right in terms of individual involvement and commitment as well as the dynamics that move a group of citizens to behave in one way as opposed to another. For example, a foolish decision is tolerated when it is made freely; that is, when a majority of the public wrongly ignores expert advice and chooses wrongly what to do, it has the option of changing its course of action and reconsidering that advice by reconstituting itself as a different majority with the power to revise previous decisions (if it is not too late). But when the public as a whole is not consulted in advance and is then forced to decide in a manner that eventually proves to be mistaken, then there is anger and resentment. These feelings are also those of betrayal—by either the expert or political leadership—and may lead to a posture that rejects offhand any leadership advice just because of its source.

It seems to me that from one perspective it is easier (even if not healthier) to relinquish one's right and power to make decisions—one's autonomy—than to hold onto that right and power and thereby take personal responsibility for choices and decisions that are potentially wrong. One's personal autonomy is accompanied by the burden of weighing reasonable options and the fear that one may not secure a successful result/outcome or the approval of others (relatives or strangers). This situation may produce a certain tension in individuals between their desire to be free to choose whatever they wish and the fear of being responsible for their autonomous decisions. One way of reducing the tension is by convincing oneself that the authority of expert leaderships, in this case, is justified and should be adhered to without reservation.

When individuals are ready to relinquish their authority to make decisions that affect them, when they are willing to let their political leaderships negotiate with an expert leadership, they must consider how their own reservations about their ability to choose correctly are applicable to all other individuals, whether members of the expert or the political leadership. On an individual level, expert communities and their leaderships cannot safeguard against mistakes, they cannot secure success and infallibility.[5] On a public level, as John S. Mill observes (1984, ch. II), the majority may be wrong, and just because it is the majority does not legitimate its choice. Coupling individual fallibility with the fallibility of groups, a leadership or a majority should alert us all to an active role of participation in decision making processes that affect us in the medical, legal, or scientific arenas.

Describing the "politicization of expertise," Dorothy Nelkin claims that "the fact that there was disagreement among experts confirmed the fears of the community and directed attention to what they felt was an arbitrary decision-making procedure in which expertise was used to mask questions of political priorities" (Nelkin 1975, 48, and also 51–54). In such cases, the public cannot feel confident in relinquishing its authority to be involved in choosing which policy is most useful or beneficial; on the contrary, public fear increases since the unmitigated trust and faith in both leaderships is shattered. This personal concern is evident not only in cases where one finds disagreement among leaders but also in cases where the leadership changes its views as if these views depended on a change in "mood" or "fashion" (see Sperber 1990). Hearing different "scientific opinions," every citizen must become responsible for taking a stand, even if the stand is not taking a stand at all.[6]

My sense, then, of the discursive exchanges taking place between the leaderships of experts and those of politicians is that they all too often overlook the importance of encouraging the personal participation of all citizens in a democratic society. Having said this, though, I do not mean to be advocating some specific sort of a liberal, libertarian, or anarchistic mode of public behavior. Instead, my concern is much more with the personal attitudes and orientation that can be fostered if all citizens are invited to participate in the games of leaderships. This does not necessarily mean that every individual must participate at every level in the public policy process. It could mean, for example, that every citizen is aware of the rules of the game played by leaderships, or that every individual feels that it is possible to change the rules of the game or devise a new game altogether. I think it possible to think of personal participation (whether in principle or in practice) as an enjoyable activity, one that depends on the participation of others and therefore is open to continuous negotiations, never sustaining a set of predetermined rules.

CHAPTER 6

Contextualizing Expertise:
Potential Empowerment

I: INTRODUCTION

Experts come in a variety of guises, as scientists who belong to professional organizations such as the BAAS, as physicians and lawyers, financial advisors and politicians, and academics of all sorts. We have seen how one group of expert scientists judges another within the hierarchical context of the BAAS (chapter 1). We have also reviewed the relations of the public, through its representatives or its majorities, with experts of different persuasions (chapters 2 and 5). But in having explored these themes concerning expertise, I have only examined historically (chapter 3) the particular expertise associated with philosophy and philosophers. At this point of the book, it may be helpful to reconsider the disciplinary context (chapter 4) that allows philosophers the freedom to explore questions about expertise from a variety of perspectives, and with a multiplicity of voices and methods.

The luxury afforded philosophers to explore the cultural settings of expertise and the possibilities for changes is often missed because of their commitments to a specific tradition or method of inquiry. Philosophers have become lamentably experts no different from those they study—with schools of thought and carefully delineated party lines and agendas. Being a philosopher by training, I think it most appropriate to conclude this book with what sociologists call a reflexive moment, one that puts my own intellectual conduct within the parameters of my critical study. With this in mind, the comments that follow are not supposed to constitute an argument in the classical sense, but instead are provided here as a recommendation for those of us who consider themselves students of the culture in which they live and think.

The recommendation is quite simple: incorporate and integrate a variety of philosophical perspectives to accomplish specified tasks, instead of engendering inter- and intradisciplinary quarrels to the extent that they will pre-empt the potential for change. This way of thinking, I admit, is at once too simple and not simple enough. Too simple in the sense of overlooking histories and differences that underlie certain ways of philosophizing; not simple enough in the sense of not specifying in detail what the next move(s) ought to be. In this respect, then, those philosophers already committed politically to a particular school may not listen to me, not even hear the story I tell. But perhaps other students, those who have not yet made up their minds or those who are disillusioned with a particular school may hear in my stories something they would like to listen to.

It is easy to be dismissive of a way of presenting ideas when the audience is not right here but is yet to come in a form of a reader. This is how utopian thinkers and cultural critics have been conveniently ignored. I plea for a critical engagement of different perspectives so that a rejection of a proposal would be based on a critical examination and not on one's prejudices. I find some urgency in my plea because I am worried that a multiplicity of critiques would set a situation wherein one critique overshadows the other and thereby licenses "mainstream" views and practices to ignore all critiques at once. Let me describe simplistically the intellectual landscape closest to my concern here.

II: A FOUR-HANDED CARD GAME

Imagine a game of bridge being played in a glass-enclosed room where you are an observer. You cannot hear a word, but because of a set of mirrors surrounding the players, their "hands" are clearly seen on a screen, and their moves and tricks are clearly denoted on the same screen. Bridge is a game of cards wherein the rules are strictly defined, but where there are a number of conventions through which the standard rules are interpreted in a variety of different, and at times incommensurable ways. To win, a team of two that sits across from each other must use the rules and conventions in ways that would reveal as much about the cards they hold as the techniques they will deploy to fulfill their contractual relationship. When the bidding is over, one team gains the privilege of announcing to all participants that a contract is established to complete a specified round of tricks. If in fact the contract is fulfilled, the team accomplishing that task is considered to have won, whereas if it falls short of fulfilling the contract, the other, silent team wins a certain amount of points.

There are four players in bridge. In my narrative about the critiques of expertise one can detect or present four players as well: Marxists, Popperians, postmodernists, and feminists. These categories or classifications are meant here in the Weberian sense of ideal types and do not correspond accurately to specific cases or texts. I think that my players are indeed playing the same game, even if their game is not usually thought of as a game of cards. I also think that they are all following similar rules, or recreating a similar set of rules. When they differ—and of course most would argue that they differ quite a bit—the difference is in their different interpretations of the rules and the conventions they establish in order to carry out their narrative techniques of articulation and their respective critiques. Unfortunately, it is not easy to pair them nor to convince them that they are engaged in the same game. For each player wants to territorialize the game, to characterize it in ways that would ensure uniqueness and appeal to different sympathies.

Some of the rules shared by Marxists, Popperians, postmodernists, and feminists are those of discursive pronouncements, wherein linguistic uses are codified and rationally articulated. In spite of Marxist critiques of bourgeois rationality, the critiques of Popperians against the abuse of reason by positivists, the critiques of postmodernists concerning the privileged position of reason in contemporary society, and the critiques of feminists that rationality is male-oriented and discriminatory to other forms of intellectual sensibilities, they all revolve their own works and explain (if no longer justify) their own positions or views through the use of rational discourse. They all "turn the tables" on traditional or canonical rationality by pushing its reign and limitations to the brink of breakdown—using rationality to oppose it, so to speak—toward the "next" possible step, however they define it.

Moreover, as individuals and in groups, all four players in the language game of contemporary culture are critics whose aim is to "expose" whatever needs exposing, "uncover" whatever layers of deceit and misrepresentation they encounter, "explain" in different ways whatever has been traditionally justified and protected from scrutiny, and "explore" different, and at times explicitly "better" ways by which to record "history" and usher a new age of intellectual and practical activity. All four envision themselves and model their positions in terms of alternatives that offer society a more accurate and helpful method and model to adopt and emulate, so as to appropriate new spaces within redefined boundaries.

Finally, in addition to the use they all make of rationality, however modified and differently used, and of the notion of critique, the four players I have in mind are simultaneously and necessarily involved in a multiplicity of games. Their concern with science, just like mine, is bound up with their concern for social and political issues, with economic conditions and the conditioning of the psyche. To discuss science is to discuss the scientific community; to discuss the scientific community is to discuss methods of inquiry and the role of leadership; to discuss these issues is to discuss social role playing, political status, and economic rewards; and to discuss these issues is to raise legal and moral questions; raising legal and moral questions brings about a discussion of personal tastes and preferences, feelings, and individual histories.

By the time these players are done analyzing anything, their work is no longer easily classified and defined: is it philosophy of science or sociology of science? Is it history of science or science economics? Does it matter how one defines the work? No, they would all have to agree. Marx the political economist is also a moralist and metaphysician; Popper the philosopher of science is also an epistemologist who cares about a "libertarian" political order; and the story goes on along these lines for postmodernists and feminists as well. That is precisely their attraction for me; that is their appeal to those involved in what one may term cultural critique or the study of cultural phenomena.

But is the "bridge" image appropriate at all? Except for the sense of bridging between language games or between predetermined boundaries, it would seem that the game of bridge is inappropriate for two main reasons. First, all four players would denounce the elitist connotation accompanying this particular bourgeois card game. Popperians would disdain the clubbishness of that particular institution, not to mention Marxists, postmodernists, and feminists. But, does their display of destain not belie their own posture as experts or individuals who have a privileged perspective, if not a privileged social status? Second, the techniques of bridge are too rigid and limited for the four players, all of whom perceive themselves to be members of the avant-garde, breaking with tradition so radically so that the very idea of having rules and conventions is rejected from the outset. Would they not claim that when rules and conventions are eventually created and mastered along "movement" or "party" lines they are at best secondary, and worse, mere imitations? It seems that without radicalism and an underground pedigree, all four players add little to the debates of the mainstream and can have no claim to change, reform, or revolution—of thought and action, of course. So, in what game can all players engage to illustrate their common concerns to replace or displace the objects of their critiques, to stress their shared background and orientation, and to minimize the casualties of intellectual sparring that would undermine their effectiveness?

Perhaps they should be playing poker. I know that there are also rules in this game, but unlike bridge, the self-stylized pronouncements of poker players are always suspect. When players ask for four cards or none, it is impossible to know what they really are holding in their hand. Facial expressions and verbal utterances are not representational in any traditional sense (and definitely unlike the verbal exchange that is established in the process of contract bridge), for they may or may not correspond to the actual cards distributed to players. The poker "bluff" is not a secondary phenomenon one can overlook or discount; it is, instead, what makes poker what it is, an interpretive game.

Now what is a bluff? To say that it is cheating is at once saying too much and too little. Too much because it imputes that everyone is bluffing and that everyone intentionally tries to mislead everyone else. This may not be the case in all games nor for all players of the same game. If anything, what makes a poker game interesting is that some do bluff while others do not, and that it is impossible to prejudge who belongs to which group. Too little because it fails to capture the intricacies of the game, the possibilities that one gambles with, and the importance of hedging one's bets. Besides, poker playing can be a means to an end, a resolution of a dispute, a means to decide who gets a coveted prize, like a horse or a ranch, or who must leave town and never dare to return. Poker is, as we have all seen so often in classical Western movies, about something other than a game of cards.

Bluffing in the present context is the process of interpretation, a process in which all players participate actively, whether they are doing something or observing the deeds of other players. Interpretation, as Socrates and Nietzsche in their respective ways have shown, is an irreducible activity whose proliferation is incessant. Not only does a word have more than one meaning, as Socrates shows time and again with notions, such as "piety" and "justice," but events are not always what they seem to be (hence the difference between appearance and reality for Plato). Nietzsche complicates the Socratic narrative, adds layers of interpretation so that he speaks of an interpretation of an interpretation, thereby opening and widening the gap between an event and its report so that any number of those conducting interpretive techniques could find their activities both helpful and elastic, in a word, bridging practices.

The label bluff can stick or have the sense of misleading only if it is possible to presuppose that the correspondence theory of meaning and truth is the prevailing standard by which to judge. Against the strictures of one-to-one correspondence, one can claim that this statement is a bluff while the other is the truth. But once this presupposition is no longer in use, to bluff is to interpret or challenge another to interpret. Bluffing here is an invitation to critically engage another in a conversation, where questions and answers, trials and dead ends, eventually lead players to agree or disagree about the status of a statement, theory, or worldview.

Unfortunately, Marxists and Popperians, for example, find their respective projects dissimilar enough not to warrant alliances and close relationships. Marxists deride Popperians for their political conservativism—the insistence on individuality and personal freedom above all other communal principles of cooperation. Popperians, in their turn, belittle the determinism commonly associated with Marxist critiques—of economic and social conditions, of the infrastructure vis-à-vis the superstructure. While advocating the necessity of having an open society, they perceive the collectivism of Marxism to be a closure in social and intellectual terms. What is lost in this family squabble is the strong self-proclamation of both Marxists and Popperians to the legitimacy of their critiques, to the superiority of their narratives over those they attempt to replace. Marxists fight classical and neoclassical economists, not so much for their models as for the bad faith in which they construct their models—the value-laden approach that eventually ends up in the production of a particular economic model that is at once misleading and self-serving. Popperians fight positivists of any affiliation, not so much for their concern with an independent reality that needs to be explained and predicted as for the methodological narrative that claims to summarize the historical record of cumulative progression from one scientific epoch to the next.

Marxists and Popperians alike are involved in interpretive debates they deem they deserve to win. Marxists and Popperians alike use the historical record differently from their opponents in order to prove their opponents wrong. They re-use whatever was available in a different way, different enough to make a radical difference in their narratives. In addition, the Marxian and Popperian narratives laid barren for a while before they could emerge and be considered as possible alternatives, as alternate narratives independent from previous ones, no matter how intimately linked they are to their predecessors in the forms of critiques. Without their claims to undermine the status quo and delegitimate its foundations, Marxists and Popperians would not enjoy the excitement of their followers. As ways of thinking, they distinguish themselves by offering something unavailable in the mainstream.

As a Marxist or Popperian one feels at once inside and outside; accepted by one's own comrades, one is immediately reminded that this acceptance is conditioned by the rejection of others, the ones who are wrong headed and misinformed, or those intentionally and maliciously working against the welfare of society. For Marxists, capitalists are not only mistaken in their view of the relationship between themselves and their workers, they are institutionally abusive and exploitive. Similarly, for Popperians, positivists are not only mistaken about the growth of scientific knowledge, they are under-mining the potential of young scientists to conjecture and explore new ideas openly and with unqualified liberty. It is in the name of liberty and progress, under the banner of political welfare and individual, psychological well-being, that Marxists and Popperians propose their critiques.

Now it may seem that even though I have moved from bridge to poker, I am still trying to pair players, pulling together Marxists and Popperians and then moving on to postmodernists and feminists. But if poker is the game, then each player is simultaneously playing alone and is part of the entire group, no matter if there are four or six play-ers. To some extent, then, whatever has been said above about Marxists and Popperians is applicable to postmodernists and fem-inists. That is, they too work with techniques of discourse that are rooted in some enlightenment notion of rationality and reason, and they too have some stock in the ideals and legacies of modes of critique. They likewise pride themselves on being inside their game, a game they created in opposition to other games, a game that invites newcomers to participate in different modes of thinking and doing, but a game that is defined by its status as being outside of the standard or mainstream games played by those who feel threatened by any form of critique.

I want to continue with the image of poker playing because it may respond to the following objections that are bound to surface from all players and other observers as well. One objection focuses on the loss of uniqueness and difference that emerges from my attempt to find common ground or shared goals and principles for all four play-ers. For example, while Marx and Popper are clearly adherents of a set of rigid principles, and their commitments are transparent and foundationalist, postmodernists pride themselves on being anti-foundationalists and having no permanent rules except for those that unfold in the activity of narrating or interpreting an event. In a similar fashion, feminists usually find common cause with Marxist critiques of the workplace, but for them gender issues are paramount in determining, for instance, the sense of injustice and alienation suf-fered in a particular factory.

I do not mean to minimize these differences nor to reduce them to one common ground and thereby rob them of their importance and specific insights. But for me what is at stake is a strategic point. Thinking and analyzing, writing and speaking are all activities that emerge from and result in activities that illustrate shifts in ori-entation not left to the theoretical domain exclusively. These shifts are to be found prominently in the political, social, economic, and legal domains. It is because of the pragmatic stakes at hand that I fear the squabbles of intellectuals and academics may result in a division of labor that unlike the Smithian ideal does not add efficiency and productivity, but undermines the possibility of setting such shifts in orientation into motion at all. Given this fear, one that can be confirmed in professional conferences and journals, it is not unreasonable to pull together these players despite their differences. This of course does not mean that they all do or will play the same game, for they are still poker players, bluffing their way around the table, interpreting themselves and others in their own unique ways, disregarding whatever is deemed worthless and paying close attention to whatever seems important to them. That level of difference is neither invaded nor overlooked from my perspective.

Another objection to lumping together disparate critiques may refer to the presumption that these players not only have similar identities (in methodological and historical terms) but also have similar goals in mind. Do feminists envision the same world order as Popperians? Is individual liberty, as Popperians understand it, not male-oriented to begin with? If so, how can feminists buy into it? To take another example, do postmodernists share the worldview of Marxists in economic terms, namely, in the sense of the public ownership of the modes of production? Would postmodernists not refuse to buy into any predetermined world order altogether? It is possible to continue and articulate an even more damning objection here concerning all the intricacies of each player in terms of the vision for which the game is played.

I do not deny that Marxists must be troubled by Popperians and vice versa, that feminists may be insulted or take issue with what either of them are concerned with, and that postmodernists may refuse to play the game of visions of a better future out of hand. But, and this is a difficult "but" to make, there still is something they all share: a profound dissatisfaction with a status quo (clearly not an identical status quo or, if identical, not perceived as identical by each group). Is this enough to make them collaborate or even partially cooperate? I believe it is! It seems that the past hundred years have not overcome the inadequacies of the age of modernity, the confusion of individuals and societies, the stupidities of leaderships, or the miscalculations of scientists and technologists. Whether the emphasis is on individuals or society, whether the focus is on science or on economic conditions, it seems that there is more to be gained by pulling together the independent forces or narratives of these players than by dividing or counterposing them.

One can even elaborate a narrative that illustrates shared traditions and legacies, shared backgrounds and histories that these four players or schools claim for themselves. But the indication of similar antecedents may turn into a reductionist move, one whereby everything has the same root(s), such as the pre-Socratic records or the Catholic doctrine, so that the distinct characteristics and influential issues are marginalized. This sort of exercise, though interesting and useful for the purpose of studying the history of ideas, for example, would not be of great service here.

III: PLAYING WITH EXPERTISE

The purpose of having the four ideal typical players I identified play the same discursive game is not in order to show common ground or conflate their different viewpoints. Instead, the purpose is to be able to use them interchangeably as I see fit without having to justify crossing any party lines. My alliances are with all of them, depending on how their techniques of explorations turn out to be useful or useless for particular purposes. Call my reading of Section F of the BAAS postmodernist (emphasizing that disciplinary differences must not lead to hierarchical ordering) or Marxist (focusing on the financial support that different sections received), Popperian (in terms of not being an "open society") or feminist (in light of the ridicule of those women who presented papers for or were in the audiences of Section F), or whatever other name may come to mind. Read my views on expertise radical or reformist, concerned with justice or with prudent political activity and behavior. Describe my philosophical orientation too leftist or not leftist enough. Regardless of any of these possibilities, I merely ask to be granted the opportunity to break beyond the codified academic and intellectual boundaries that confine one to be identified with this or that group but not both. As far as I am concerned, these different groups of players are all playing discursive games that intersect. I and my work are consciously positioned at points of intersection, where there is more than one game being played at once, where more than one discourse can be used strategically to critically engage a theory, model, or practice.

When more than one discourse is being used at once, one may charge, there is confusion and chaos. Is confusion and chaos not the life we lead daily, wherein we all use multiple discourses without losing our self-identity or sanity, or where we occasionally lose both but know under what conditions they can be reclaimed? When I speak to students in a paternalistic manner and thereby do injustice to their dignity and autonomy within the university setting, I can redeem my behavior and adjust it to fit the game and its rules. When I treat my young child as if she were a college student and expect of her intellectual parity with me, it is obvious that I confuse one discourse with another, applying an inappropriate set of rules and expectations to her detriment. The same can be said of the four discourses used by Marxists, Popperians, postmodernists, and feminists. They are all context-bound but have edges elastic enough to allow an expansion or contraction.

Each discourse can be developed in isolation from all others, but each can be used simultaneously with others as well. One can move in and out of discursive practices, engage only parts of them, play only one hand. I gave myself, then, self-licensure to carry out a critical examination of expertise and the various critical discourses that deal with its practices and consequences. Self-licensure has been understood in contemporary critiques as empowerment, the process through which individuals, whether the proletariat or women of color, find a way to be noticed and heard, to make a difference and have an impact on their own lives and those of others. Empowerment at one level is nothing more nor less than a self-proclamation, the license one gives to oneself without appeal to anyone else. But at another level empowerment requires an articulation of the conditions under which such self-proclamation is possible in reference to power relations. To encourage someone to take charge, as some how-to psychological manuals do, is meaningless and useless because it is not that simple (even though or perhaps because it seems too simple). What else is needed to make that shift in orientation?

Here is where things get complex, because of the multiplicity of possible strategies one could use. Marxists commonly emphasize economic conditions as the essential ones to be changed in order to permit empowerment of any sort. Without transforming material conditions, they contend, there will never be more than lip service paid to actual empowerment of individuals. Feminists contend, along similar lines, that without the transformation of gender relations as they manifest themselves in every aspect of our lives, the notion of empowerment will remain nothing more than a theoretical construct. Popperians contend that without the transformation of the conditions under which scientific and technological research is undertaken, there is no sense of speaking of the empowerment of individuals who wish to participate in the activities of the scientific community. And postmodernists, for their part, contend that without transforming cultural conditions, those of social relations as well as linguistic ones, it makes no sense to discuss empowerment.

I may be overstating or oversimplifying the case of empowerment, for all four groups of critics speak of empowerment, even though none can identify a complete transformation of the conditions with which they are concerned. Yet, for all four, even the partial changes they observe give sufficient hope that complete transformation is possible (no matter how long it takes) and that the discussion of empowerment will not remain an idle intellectual activity. The question, then, may turn out to be for all of them whether empowerment is a *telos* or an ideal to strive for or, instead, a regulative ideal one works with all along without expecting it ever to be fully achieved. Each group and individuals within these groups find their own responses to this question. The answers are diverse enough not to warrant a summary or a reduction into one answer. But, no matter what the response turns out to be, it seems to me that the actualization of the notion of empowerment will benefit from adding the following dimension.

When coupling the notion of empowerment and its actualization with the notion of responsibility in an attempt to illustrate to what extent they are manageable and within the reach of every individual, I speak of nothing short of a revolutionary or radical way of looking at the world in which we live. This is not to say that such attempts have not been undertaken before or that all such attempts have failed so far, and that therefore my own discussion will lead the way where no way has been found of late. This would be presumptuous and wrong. If anything, the four "philosophies" or "movements" I discuss here all participate in and are valuable models for doing exactly this.

When using postmodernism to examine the social role of experts, I invoke certain Popperian/Marxist/feminist arguments and positions that undermine the standard view concerning the validity of scientific theories and models. But why rehearse this way of dealing with expertise? Would it not suffice to warn people about experts and advise them not to believe in their suggestions unconditionally? And if it turns out that a warning is not enough, why is it the case?, and what else can one do to insert suspicion where none existed before? I will answer these four questions in turn by emphasizing the connection (discussed in chapter 2) between epistemology and psychology.

First, the rehearsal of the positions that attempt to cast suspicion on the activities and claims of scientists is never redundant or overdone. Since scientists are still the heroes of our culture and still enjoy privileged status, anything that contributes to the challenge of that status must be reiterated. This is not in order to eliminate scientists from having any role in our culture, only to curtail their pronouncements, contextualize their verdicts, and require them to be accountable to the audience that listens to their proposals. Besides, science is still the way by which most people conceive of the realities that surround them. When these realities are questioned, there is plenty of room to question many other things, such as social relations or the political power of one group versus another. In short, the challenge of science is a necessary (but of course not a sufficient) step on the way to reconsider power relations.

Second, what does it mean to warn someone about something? A warning issued by an individual carries with it the force exerted by that individual. The force may be that of panic, when someone yells "fire!" and you react instinctively and without regard if the person yelling is a firefighter—an expert—or a passerby. But the force may be based on the credentials and qualifications associated with the individual issuing the warning. For example, the warning of a nuclear physicist about a possible meltdown carries with it a stronger persuasive force than the same one if issued by me. But here is the rub: is my warning concerning expertise, as expressed in this book, dependent on my own expertise? If so, am I not guilty of playing one sort of expertise against another? If guilty, does such a technique or strategy not violate my own warning not to accept or remain skeptical about expert warnings?

Third, it seems that warnings as such are not helpful. They end up being stacked up, one after the other, one on top of the other, on one's desk or in one's mind, without having the sort of practical impact they are meant to have. So, the warning may begin with an epistemological position or posture, but it must become practical and personal. The reason why some of the chapters in this book and especially the present one move toward psychology is that I intend to reach the reader on a personal as well as on an intellectual level. But how can I get to you? I can tell you stories, engage you in my telling of the stories, upset or entertain you, and perhaps even get you to respond by writing nasty or friendly comments in the margins of the book, deciding to write a review of this book, or enticing you to write a different book about the same topics.

Fourth, in this respect, the examination of personal relationships in the BAAS (e.g., Galton's family connections) and the discussion of responsibility and empowerment are devices through which to personalize the book. As interpretive narratives, they serve to reach a readership that may be touched by something that is said or told in a manner different from previous ones. I have no illusion that my narratives do not remain philosophical in the sense of being overly jargonized and at times obtuse. Yet, I have consciously tried to transfer the narratives into individual cases and personal accounts so that the reader might identify with or be appalled by a situation. It remains, of course, an open question how successful my trials have been in each particular case.

To some extent what I am advocating here is a psychological overhaul. That is, to think of one's responsibility regarding self-empowerment is a task that is accomplished by envisioning a (completely?) different set of circumstances from those that are currently in place so that the possibility of empowerment can be actualized. This sort of undertaking, psychologically speaking, is doubtlessly most difficult. Is such an overhaul worth the effort? In one sense, the answer is clearly no, for the mere promise of a possible empowerment is not worth the effort that goes into a psychological overhaul. In another sense, though, the answer is yes, for without an attempt to overhaul one's psyche, there may never arise the possibility of empowerment.

Let us assume that it is worth pursuing the adventure of a psychological overhaul. What would such an activity entail? What precisely does it take to radically change one's psychological outlook on life? To begin with, it means not to take anything for granted, to feel a void very close to one's forehead, to reconsider every item stored in one's consciousness and subconsciousness, and to expect nothing from others and oneself. Is it possible to function in such a state of mind? I would guess that most therapists, using their collective, clinical data and experiences, would claim that it is impossible to function "normally" (socially?) under these severe conditions of utter confusion and lack of an environmental reality within which to anchor one's personality and relationships. But what if Spinoza's notion of "peace of mind" was added into the equation?

You see, I can be as confused as I want, not being able to rely on any point of reference whatsoever. As long as this state of mind, this condition of mine is sanctioned by myself, authorized, if you wish, then it is not frightening or alienating at all, for it has been my choice to be in that condition. The self-recognition of my choice and the sanctioning that it receives from me is what allows me to be at peace with myself. I contend that self-induced confusion, if it is a means for the accomplishment of an end found worthy by me (in this case, empowerment), would be welcomed and maintain a psychological peace and stability.

As you are reading these last few passages, you may be nodding to yourself and saying: but how does the "empowered" individual relate to those still "unempowered?" It is in part an issue of being an example to others, offering others to join you, but not an imposition. You may continue and say, well, it may be true for a few strong personalities, but how can one generalize from a few cases to the population at large? I cannot dispute this objection, for I have not experimented with these ideas enough to see the results in any generalizable manner. Yet, I would like you to entertain the idea, the possibility of this idea being practical, and figure out for yourself the parameters under which such personal experimentation could be useful.

To predetermine the conditions and variables under which

empowerment becomes possible would violate my sense of contingencies and my own open-ended view of the world and its inhabitants. If anything, I am not an expert on these matters who can provide you with a chronology of events; I can only try in my own peculiar ways to experiment with a process of empowerment. Perhaps my own vocabulary is not "fit" to speak about these things because I overlook certain cultural factors that preempt such an experimentation or that make such an experimentation too risky for most individuals. Perhaps the language of empowerment will develop simultaneously with the rules and principles that will guide it and thereby would require a cultural change far greater than anticipated here. If either the rules or the language are precast, the entire process may never get off the ground. What can help the process along, from my perspective, are some personal attempts and trials (at first) by those who can afford personal risks that may prove helpful to others who contemplate empowerment but for whom the stakes are too high.

IV: THE FOUR PLAYERS CONTINUE

A feminist critique of expertise may look different from a Popperian critique, and a Marxist critique will stress different aspects from a postmodernist one. Yet, they all share a suspicion of that privileged group of people, the so-called self-proclaimed experts, whose influence and power are so immense in the present cultural context that they cannot be ignored nor left alone to police and explain themselves. My own critical review of expertise is linked to the views of science and technology expressed differently by Marxists, Popperians, postmodernists, and feminists. They have all contributed to a literature on the status of science and technology in the modern world in ways that require an examination of well-accepted ideas about expert knowledge and about the assumptions that are taken for granted when these questions are raised. They are all philosophical in the sense of taking nothing for granted and probing as much as their linguistic techniques allow them the depths and breadths of the cultural parameters under and within which the activities of experts are perceived.

I do not expect members of all these four groups to be fully satisfied with my efforts, for they can each find deficiency in this or that specific use of a technique or method of inquiry. My own study is probably not feminist, Marxist, postmodern, or Popperian enough for the guardians of these respective faiths. In my own defense, I say that I do not accept any of these modes of intellectual and practical productions as faiths, and therefore need not be a disciple or a believer. Instead, I take them as tools that are sometimes better not used at all for they cannot "do the job" as well as it can be done with other tools, or as tools one gets bored with or tired of using. This attitude is neither degrading nor "disrespectful" (as some of my writings have been accused of being). The engagement of a tool is an act of respect. It is with this orientation that I offer my reflections to others, as an invitation to rethink and re-do what has already been said and done.

The engagement of ideas and practices as tools is already introduced in chapter 3, where I examined the myth of expertise. The expertise we are left with at this juncture is bound by a set of circumstances that contextualize its use or deployment. Such an expertise can be thought of as Expertise (with a capital E) or as expertise (with lower case e). When Expertise is used, it is a bound variable, a temporal point of intersection in which indeed it reigns supreme, that is, all the criteria and judgments in that situation are fully dependent on it. For example, during back surgery, the expertise of a surgeon is what defines the success or failure of the operation. Under these conditions, at this particular moment, the expertise of a surgeon is the supreme adjudicator of what should and should not be done. But to shift from that moment to another is a shift of circumstances as well so that the surgical expertise then becomes an expertise that may no longer be applicable at all.

Once expertise is thought of in terms of tools and instruments as opposed to the privilege it may assume in theoretical terms, then its status is open to changes all the time. The changes themselves cannot always be predetermined for they depend on the context in or for which they change. And expertise is a moving target, too, whose credentials and position cannot be fastened once and for all to a particular set of foundations.

There is no finality to our activity either as experts or the users of expertise, only points of arrival and departure, meeting points, and empty points. Some points we skip, some we stay at for a long time, some we hope to reach, and others we resent. But the open-ended movement from one point to another is not fruitless, for the conditions that push us from one to another are instructive and in constant change. Can we change these conditions themselves? At times we can, at others we feel overwhelmed by their seeming predetermination and rigidity. No matter how we feel, the very fact that we feel something is already an indication that we are engaged in the activity of change, even if only marginally or helplessly and at a distance. The question of responsibility surfaces at this juncture once again.

To be engaged is to make a statement. Statements have authors whose responsibility is tied to the authority these statements eventually carry with them. This is true whether or not the authors are experts. So, the distinguishing characteristic of experts is not their authority but that their authority has been perceived as privileged vis-à-vis the authority of others. The privilege, as pointed throughout this book, has been linked to the validity of science and technology (even for physicians or academics) as a privileged epistemological position in comparison to all other forms of expression. Once that privilege is undermined, as I have tried to do in every chapter, other privileges will be questioned, too. Without any privilege, the statements and declarations of experts are just as valuable or silly—susceptible to challenges—as those of all other citizens. The price, one would object, of this position may be too high, for it would obliterate the differences that can be detected between scientific and nonscientific narratives. This price or cost is worth paying, as far as I am concerned, because there seems to be only a superficial difference and not, as some presume, a profound one.

V: THE EXPERTISE OF LISTENING

Listening to oneself, one need not be alone or be speaking at all. Rather, one may find another person or text that speaks in the way one would like to speak or would have liked to have spoken. When we listen, then, we consider what we want to say, even if we are in no position to make our ideas known publicly or even to a small audience. We search for and listen to those who express our views and opinions or to those views and ideas that we evaluate as agreeable. So, when we turn to scientific experts, when they speak and pronounce their verdicts, all that we are looking for is a confirmation of what we would have said had we been in their place.

When telling a postmodern story of listening, one may speak of oracles or of the accounts of scientific experts and/or their translators, philosophers of science. But who are those philosophers of science? Are they necessarily translators? And what is the translation they offer? Just as scientific experts are exposed in narratives, such as the one about Section F of the BAAS, so that their presumed privilege is critically scrutinized, philosophers of science, such as Popperians, can be exposed as well. The exposition of philosophers of science parallels that of scientists, for in both cases the issue is translation or more precisely a translation that privileges science.

As noted above, the four-hand poker game played by Marxists, Popperians, postmodernists, and feminists illustrates the untenability of prescribing a privileged position to a unique scientific or philosophical translation, interpretation, or narrative. At best, one can speak of a multiplicity of translations, interpretations, and narratives, each of which is context-bound so that each contextual reading assumes a certain pragmatic purpose for which it is undertaken. In this sense, then, the question of listening to experts takes on a fairly personal character.

Regardless if one adopts a Popperian orientation of piecemeal engineering toward the growth of knowledge and the critical devices by which it is scrutinized and revised, a Lyotardian attitude of interpretive experimentation toward all textual expressions, a Marxist approach that acknowledges historical contingencies in all epistemological affairs and decisions, or a feminist concern with gender discrimination in the construction and distribution of knowledge in general, one is confronted with a choice. The "world"—"reality" or "ideas"—is no longer presented as a unified, systematic model one can apprehend and comprehend once and for all. Instead, *the* world is presented as *a* world that exists alongside other worlds. The world as we know it has been fragmented and dispersed into contingent pieces, so that each individual can choose to listen to more than one voice at the same time.

All four groups, as described above, contribute to the dissemination of scientific authority in their respective ways. Their contributions undermine our ability to listen to a single voice of scientific authority or, for that matter, to any voice that claims permanent or foundational authority. Once we find ourselves in this situation, we have to listen to a variety of voices, including our own. What does our voice say? Perhaps nothing, for it is not accustomed to speak about certain matters. So, the introspection I recommend—listening to one's own voice—turns out to be an alignment with another's voice, whomever one chooses as a voice worthy of listening to. The process of listening may be short or long, it may change radically or not at all; these variables will depend on the specific circumstances when an advice is sought, when a "listening" happens.

Can my recommendation to listen to others' expertise as knowledge that is qualified and has only temporal authority withstand the standard criticisms of relativism and skepticism? Probably yes, for the following reasons. My view does not eliminate resort to expertise; it only warns one of using expertise beyond contextual and pragmatic confines one can determine for oneself. Moreover, though endorsing a skeptical orientation toward all knowledge claims, my view does not undercut the possibility of knowing with a great deal of certainty something specific in a particular case. And finally, to discount the permanence of expertise or its ahistorical pretensions is not the same as discounting expertise in temporal terms. There are situations where expertise is useful and fruitful, where one cannot do without it. But the very existence of such situations does not thereby legitimate an appeal to expertise in all other situations. And here the tables are turned once again toward the user, the reader, the listener, to engage the situation in a way that allows a choice, that empowers and is empowering. The price, as said before, may have to be assessed psychologically, but the switch to the psychological from the epistemological in and of itself should not be seen as a deterrent.

NOTES TO CHAPTER 1

1. One may argue that Susan Faye Cannon (1978), especially in chapters 6 and 7, provides a different interpretation regarding the launching of Section F in terms of what the founders expected to accomplish. In light of Cannon's reading one may appreciate how closely Ingram's defense agrees with the "original intent" of Whewell, Richard Jones, and other founders.

2. Morrell and Thackray (1981, 31) indicate that in spite of the differences between the two organizations, there are numerous similarities. "The Royal Society, founded in 1660, became the vehicle through which a group of moderate Anglicans was able to express its views of nature and of society. . . . The parallels with the British Association are immediate and intriguing. The Royal Society was conceived just after the Civil War and Commonwealth, when Britain underwent her last revolution in recent history. The only other period of troubles of comparable severity in modern British life lies in the 1830s and 1840s with their religious sectarianism, political party reconstruction, and intense class feeling. In these decades a similar group of moderate Anglicans presided over the successful development of the only other great central presiding power that British science has known."

3. Morrell and Thackray (1981, 94): "The triumphant success of the York Meeting launched the British Association for the Advancement of Science on its long career. As Harcourt himself was to put it two decades later, the credit for proposing to build a craft on which 'the united crew of British science might sail' lay with Brewster. But it was to be Harcourt who took up the proposal and over the course of the next several years 'manned the ship . . . constructed her charts, and piloted the vessel.' . . ."

4. One can write an entire study devoted to a comparison between the British and American Associations not only in terms of the motivation for their formation and their institutional structure, but also in terms of the kinds of debates that ensued in both regarding the criteria for scientific credibility. Parallel to Morrell and Thackray's study of the formation of the BAAS is Sally Gregory Kohlstedt's work (1976) that studies the formation of the AAAS.

5. According to Morrell and Thackray (1981, 32), science is "the dominant mode of cognition of industrial society. The deliberate creation of boundaries between natural and religious or political knowledge, the conceptualization of science as a sharply edged and value-neutral domain of knowledge, the subordination of the biological and social to the physical sciences, the harnessing of a rhetoric of science, technology, and progress—these were some of the ways in which an ideology of science was constructed."

6. The focus on sections and their formation is no small matter, even if it appears at first to be a bureaucratic issue alone. As noted in the case of the formation of the AAAS, the circumvention of forming formal sections with their own presidents and officers enhanced the concentration of power in the hands of few "leaders" who constituted a Standing Committee that in fact ruled on any scientific paper delivered during the entire annual meeting, either on the question of acceptance or on the question of inclusion and publication in the *Proceedings* (Kohlstedt 1976, 178–179).

7. Morrell and Thackray (1981, 292): "BAAS statisticians were simply to produce the quantitative data from which in the indefinite future some statistical Kepler might induce the true laws of political economy. Statisticians were to register what existed, and not to suggest what ought to exist by providing remedies for dire social problems."

8. William Farr, in his report of the committee that examined the proposal to discontinue Section F, discusses this financial aspect.

9. Henderson (1973, 329): "Most economists credit A. A. Cournot with the first mathematical statement of the concept of demand elasticity. Similarly, the Giffen paradox is most commonly associated with Alfred Marshall's *Principles of Economics*. Yet, William Whewell, a British philosopher and mathematician, published a mathematical statement of the elasticity concept in 1829, nine years before the appearance of Cournot's *Researches*, using the demand elasticity coefficient as a device to identify Giffen goods in 1850, forty-five years before Alfred Marshall." It should be noted in this context that Whewell's novelty is created by Henderson's interpretation, but is cleared up by the perusal of Whewell's original texts. There it becomes clear he was not trying to formalize the "elasticity of demand," but rather to mathematicize Ricardo's system in order to show it internally inconsistent.

10. Henderson (1986, 385) argues that: "The cornerstone of Cambridge education under Whewell was the methodological tradition of Newton and Bacon. In Whewell's view, their inductive methodology was also the appropriate approach to the study of the social sciences. Induction was something more than mere description of phenomena or data gathering by means of either experimentation or careful and complete observation. A crucial step was the introduction of a new conception which evolved out of the gathering and study of information."

11. Koot (1980, 203–204) concludes his essay by saying: "The significance of English historical economics does not lie chiefly in the issue of methodology. This was sometimes admitted by both sides . . . The conflict was partly political. . . . The dispute was also partly due to differing estimates of the importance of history in the study of the social sciences. Further, the conflict was also fueled by personal disputes, competition for academic posts, and divergent opinions on the proper role of economists in society. Most importantly, however, the dispute was partly a consequence of nearly opposite views on the question whether economics was a science or an art. . . . The historical economists did serve as a constant reminder to Marshall's school that the conclusions of scientific economic analysis were hypothetical, and thus that the formulation of public policy ought to grant a larger role to induction—i.e., historical research." See also John Maloney (1985, 116), who claims that there are three different levels of examining the British historical school: Was it a united group? What proportion of combination of induction and deduction are preferred? And was the group epistemologically similar to or different from the Marshallians?

12. Galton's pamphlet and Farr's response to it are in file No. 159 "Annual Meetings, Plymouth, 1877" of the BAAS Archives, Bodleian Library, Oxford University, Oxford, U.K. (References below are to Pamphlet.) The published record is in the *Journal of the Statistical Society* (1877), XL:468–476.

13. Just as political economy is used here as a case study for the purpose of evaluating the criteria by which scientists were granted expert status and the means by which they validated their findings, one could examine Galton's development of the theory of eugenics—especially since it has become a focus of many controversies regarding Nazi views of race purity and identification (and the extermination of millions of people in light of these "scientific findings") to contemporary policies about criminal rehabilitation programs and supplements to education program, such as Headstart for young students, not to mention various other political debates regarding race relations from apartheid in South Africa to civil rights in the U.S. (e.g., Chase 1980, Lifton 1986).

14. Pearson's assessment of Galton's importance as a scientist is compromised by the reference to Galton's eugenics (1922, 22–23). See also MacKenzie (1981, 51): "It is my argument that Galton's eugenics was tied in two ways to the social group to which he belonged. First, Galton's early eugenics theorizing drew on his social experience as a resource, the form of his eugenics thought reflecting the form of organization of his social group, and at the same time legitimating it. Second, his eugenics can very clearly be seen as part of the wider movement in thought known as scientific naturalism—a movement that has been analyzed as expressing the social interests of scientific professionals."

15. In this context, it may be interesting to note that the sexism exhibited by Galton is not limited, at that period, to the BAAS, but found its way to the AAAS. See, for example, the refusal to formally discuss membership of women in the AAAS until 1859 (eleven years after the formation of the AAAS) and the fact that by 1860 there were only three women members. It is odd, though, that the AAAS's leadership refers to the BAAS as having progressive policies concerning the encouragement of participation by women in their annual meetings, charging only half price of regular fees (Kohlstedt 1976, 103).

NOTES TO CHAPTER 3

1. Plato, *The Last Days of Socrates*, trans. by Hugh Tredennick (New York: Penguin Books, 1954). This translation elaborates on the example of the horse, unlike the two other versions: (1) *Socrates' Defense* in Plato, *The Collected Dialogues*, eds. Edith Hamilton and Huntington Cairns (Princeton, N.J.: Princeton University Press, 1961), and (2) *The Trial and Death of Socrates*, translated by G. M. A. Grube (Indianapolis: Hackett Publishing Co., 1975).

2. Feyerabend makes this claim about the propaganda-like quality of Galileo's work (Feyerabend 1975, ch. 9).

NOTES TO CHAPTER 4

1. A sense of the narrowness of contemporary conceptions concerning the relations of economics and psychology is displayed in two entries, "psychology and economics" and "psychology and political economy" in *The New Palgrave: A Dictionary of Economics* published in 1987 as a sequel to the one published in 1910. While the former entry was written for the 1987 edition and stresses the narrowness of the relation, the latter, written by Wicksteed in 1910 (and reprinted in 1933), is much broader in its concerns. For example, terms such as "risk/benefit analysis," "game theory," and the "information revolution" are dominant in the recent entry, while the concern over the very nature of economic theory, whether or not it had become nothing but "applied psychology" dominates Wicksteed's entry.

2. Cf. Malcolm Rutherford: "while the psychology used in economics is implicit, it nevertheless deeply affects the nature of economic reasoning," (Earl 1988, 38).

3. Lawrence Boland, who helped clarify the methodological concerns of economists in Popperian terms, believes that one should not narrow the discussion of the foundations and prospects of psychological economics to the integration of psychology and economics. Boland, the pluralistic

methodologist, proves once again that pluralism is the only way in which psychological economics can avoid a future crisis of identity. Instead of worrying about the proper integration or the level of interdependence or even the amount of necessary reductionism between the two disciplines, Boland invites economists to consider the insights of philosophers and sociologists as well. Cf. Lawrence A. Boland, "Individualist Economics Without Psychology" (Earl 1988, 167).

4. Though some historians of psychology, such as Raymond H. Wheeler (1929) and Richard Lowry (1971), trace the development of psychology to the seventeenth century, John Flugel makes a convincing argument for emphasizing the scientific development of psychology from the 1830s (Flugel 1951).

5. For a comprehensive discussion of the theoretical status and relation of psychology and neuroscientific research see Robert N. McCauley (1986).

6. For a further examination of the question of disciplinary boundaries, see "Symposium on crossdisciplinarity" in *Social Epistemology*, Vol. 4, No. 3, July–September 1990, pp. 259–321.

7. The mathematical twist given to the utilitarian principles of Bentham and Mill as applied to economics is discussed by Francis Y. Edgeworth in his entry "Probability" in the *Encyclopedia Britannica* (1910, 379).

8. Adam Smith's analysis of power-relations within the capitalist marketplace are "Marxist," and thus identify economics as an ideological exercise veiled in the garbs of rationality, when he asserts that the workers will always find themselves at a disadvantageous positions when confronted by their employers, the capitalists (see Smith 1937, pp. 66–69, 249–250).

9. Cf. William Stanley Jevons (1958); in spite of his promotion of mathematical empirical laws, see his disclaimers vis-à-vis the inductivists, such as John S. Mill, pp. 752ff.

10. When Popper discusses the danger of psychologism in the context of examining social theories (sociology), his warning is against reductionism because he believes that it will deprive sociology of its autonomy. His remarks about the social sciences also include economics at least in the sense of the concept of "economic man." For Popper, then, there is no difference between methodological and ontological reduction (Popper 1962, II, ch. 14: "The Autonomy of Sociology", 89–99).

11. One of the most vocal advocate of this view of the autonomy of economics is George J. Stigler, "The Influence of Events and Policies on Economic Theory" (Stigler 1965, 30). Regardless of his view of economics as applied psychology during the age of Menger and the Austrian School, Schumpeter agrees with Hume and Smith that the reliance of economics on psychology should not be conceived as depriving economics of its independence (Cf. Schumpeter 1954, 27–28, 446–448).

NOTES TO CHAPTER 5

1. When speaking of a scientific leadership of experts, Stich and Nisbett, for example, are concerned to link these individuals to a specific "cognitive authority" that warrants these people's position and to which the public is prepared to defer (Stich and Nisbett 1984, 237). In general, then, Stich and Nisbett concur with a general public sentiment that there are such individuals who are called "experts," that these individuals have a certain esteemed position in the public mind, and that such a position is justified on epistemological grounds. But when a "cognitive conservative" meets a "cognitive rebel," whose opinion carries more authority? The answer to this question is no longer simply an epistemological one, but either political (Stich and Nisbett 1984, 239–240) or sociological (Gilbert and Mulkay 1984). Once again, the political grounds of discussion, democratic or others, as illustrated above, are somehow not only linked to epistemological disputes as secondary factors but must supplement them when there is no final court of appeals.

2. The question of "limited resources" or the notion of "scarcity" as an important presupposition for arguments such as Stigler's is critically reviewed in Sassower (1991b).

3. On the issue of expert disagreement, more specifically on the question of the integrity of science and the reliability of the scientific method in light of contradictory expert witness testimony as noted already in nineteenth century England (see Hamlin 1986 and Fuller 1988, III, ch. 9: "The Elusiveness of Consensus in Science").

4. David Young, for instance, documenting the abuse of professional, occupational licensing in America, argues that "contrary to the assertions of professional groups, the public welfare is rarely advanced [by] these laws [of licensure]" (Young 1987, 2). Echoing the concerns of Milton Friedman in general terms (Friedman 1962, Ch. 9), of Jethro Lieberman in terms of experts (Lieberman 1970, Ch. 2), and of Thomas Szasz in terms of psychoanalysis (Szasz 1974), Young suggests that the public cannot trust professional organizations even when they claim to take into consideration public concerns. Professional organizations as scientific communities do not always (if ever) monitor themselves so that public interests and not the interests of experts will be served by the advice and practice of specialists. As such, these communities fail to approximate the sort of goals suggested by Russell and Bohr.

5. One of the clearest attempts to provide a formal method by which the public can approach (and eventually decide and choose among) conflicting scientific and technical questions or advice in order to formulate policies is found in Roberts, Thomas, and Dowling 1984.

6. Expert advice is used, according to Nelkin, to legitimize political plans and reinforce existing positions; however, whenever there is a disagreement among experts, the political conflict is bound to increase and the political impact of experts is bound to decrease (Nelkin 1975, 51–54).

REFERENCES

Adorno, Theodor W. (1973), *The Jargon of Authenticity* [1964], trans. K. Tarnowski and F. Will. Evanston: Northwestern University Press.

Agassi, Joseph. (1981), *Science and Society, Studies in the Sociology of Science*. Dordrecht, Holland: D. Reidel Publishing.

———. (1985), *Technology: Philosophical and Social Aspects*. Dordrecht, Holland: D. Reidel Publishing.

———. (1986), "The Politics of Science," *Journal of Applied Philosophy* 3:35–48.

———. (1990), "Democratizing Medicine," *In Prescriptions: the Dissemination of Medical Authority*, eds. G. Ormiston and R. Sassower. Westport, CT: Greenwood Press, 3–22.

Arkes, Hal R., and Kenneth R. Hammond. (1986), *Judgment and Decision Making: An Interdisciplinary Reader*. Cambridge: Cambridge University Press.

Becher, Harvey William. (1971), *William Whewell and Cambridge Mathematics*. Ph.D. diss., University of Missouri at Columbia.

Becker, Gary S. (1964), *Human Capital: A Theoretical and Empirical Analysis*. New York: National Bureau of Economic Research.

———. (1976), *The Economic Approach to Human Behavior*. Chicago: University of Chicago Press.

Bett, Richard. (1989), "The Sophists and Relativism," *Phronesis*, XXXIV/2, pp. 139–169.

Bledstein, Burton J. (1978), *Culture of Professionalism: The Middle Class and the Development of Higher Education in America*. New York: W. W. Norton.

Bohr, Niels. (1955), "Analysis and Synthesis in Science," in Otto Neurath, Rudolf Carnap, and Charles Morris, eds., *Foundations of the Unity of Science: Toward an International Encyclopedia of Unified Science*, Vol. 1. Chicago and London: University of Chicago Press.

Bonar, James. (1924), *Malthus and his Work*. New York: Macmillan.

British Association for the Advancement of Science, Annual Reports. London: John Murray. The dates of these Reports are one year after the Meeting. (References to BAASR date the Report and not the Meeting.)

Campbell, T. D. (1971), *Adam Smith's Science of Morals*. Totowa, NJ: Rowman and Littlefield.

Cannon, Susan Faye. (1978), *Science in Culture: The Early Victorian Period*. New York: Dawson and Science History Publications.

Chase, Allan. (1980), *The Legacy of Malthus: The Social Costs of the New Scientific Racism*. Urbana, IL: University of Illinois Press.

Coats, A. W. (1954), "The Historist Reaction in English Political Economy 1870–90," *Economics* XXI:143–53.

Collingridge, David, and Colin Reeve. (1986), *Science Speaks to Power: The Role of Experts in Policymaking*. New York: St. Martin's Press.

de Condorcet, Antoine-Nicolas. (1979), *Sketch for a Historical Picture of the Progress of the Human Mind* [1795], trans. June Barraclough. Westport, CT: Greenwood Press.

Dahl, Robert A. (1982), *Dilemmas of Pluralist Democracy: Autonomy Vs. Control.* New Haven and London: Yale University Press.

Darwin, Charles. (1859), *The Origin of Species by Means of Natural Selection or The Preservation of Favoured Races in the Struggle for Life.* New York: Avenel Books.

Deleuze, Gilles, and Felix Guattari. (1986), *Kafka: Toward a Minor Literature* [1975], trans. by D. Polan. Minneapolis: University of Minnesota Press.

Dewey, John. (1960), *The Quest for Certainty: A Study of the Relation of Knowledge and Action* [1929]. New York: Capricorn Books.

Earl, Peter E., ed. (1988), *Psychological Economics.* Boston: Kluwer Academic Publishers.

Dhombres, Jean. (1988), "Science and Anti-Science: An Old Story," *Impact of Science on Society.* Vol. 38, no. 2, 209–217.

Dickson, David. (1984), *The New Politics of Science.* New York: Pantheon Books.

Edgeworth, Francis Y. (1910), "Probability," *Encyclopedia Britannica.* 11th ed. Cambridge: Cambridge University Press.

Faust, David. (1984), *The Limits of Scientific Reasoning.* Minneapolis: University of Minnesota Press.

Feyerabend, Paul. (1975), *Against Method: Outline of an Anarchistic Theory of Knowledge.* London: Verso.

———. (1978), *Science in a Free Society.* London: NLB.

Flugel, John C. (1951), *A Hundred Years of Psychology.* 2nd ed. London: Gerald Duckworth.

Foley, Vernard. (1976), *The Social Physics of Adam Smith.* West Lafayette, IN: Purdue University Press.

Friedman, Milton. (1953), "The Methodology of Positive Economics," *Essays in Positive Economics*. Chicago: The University of Chicago Press.

———. (1962), *Capitalism and Freedom*. Chicago: University of Chicago Press.

Fuller, Steve. (1988), *Social Epistemology*. Indianapolis: Indiana University Press.

Galton, Francis. (1877), "Pamphlet," file No.159, "Annual Meetings, Plymouth, 1877," BAAS Archives, Bodleian Library, Oxford University, U.K.

———. (1908), *Memories of My Life*. London: Methuen and Co.

Gellner, Ernest (1974), *Legitimation of Belief.* Cambridge: Cambridge University Press.

Gilbert, G. Nigel, and Michael Mulkay. (1984), *Opening Pandora's Box: A Sociological Analysis of Scientists' Discourse*. Cambridge: Cambridge University Press.

Gould, Stephen Jay, and Niles Eldredge. (1977), "Punctuated Equilibria: The Tempo and Mode of Evolution Reconsidered," *Paleobiology*, Vol. 3, 115–151.

Habermas, Jürgen. (1975), *Legitimation Crisis*, trans. by Thomas McCarthy. Boston: Beacon Press.

Hamlin, Christopher. (1986), "Scientific Method and Expert Witnessing: Victorian Perspectives on a Modern Problem," *Social Studies of Science*, Vol. 16, 485–513.

Hegel, G. W. F. (1974), *Lectures on the History of Philosophy*, trans. E. S. Haldale, and F. H. Simson. New York: Humanities Press.

Held, David, and Christopher Pollitt. (1986), *New Forms of Democracy*. Beverly Hills, CA: Sage Publications.

Henderson, James P. (1973), "William Whewell's Mathematical Statements of Price Flexibility, Demand Elasticity and the Giffen Paradox," *The Manchester School of Economic and Social Studies*, 3:329–42.

———. (1986), "Sir John William Lubbock's On Currency—'an interesting book by a still more interesting man,'" *History of Political Economy*, 18:383–404.

Hirshleifer, J. (1977), "Economics from a Biological Viewpoint," *The Journal of Law and Economics*, XX:1–52.

Hofstadter, Richard. (1955), *Social Darwinism in American Thought* [1944]. Boston: Beacon Press.

———. (1962), *Anti-Intellectualism in American Life*. New York: Knopf.

Hollander, Samuel. (1983), "William Whewell and John Stuart Mill on the Methodology of Political Economy," *Studies in History and Philosophy of Science*, 14:127–68.

Howarth, O. J. R. (1931), *The British Association for the Advancement of Science: A Retrospect 1831–1931*. London: British Association for the Advancement of Science.

Jevons, William Stanley. (1965), *The Theory of Political Economy* [1965]. New York: A. M. Kelley.

———. (1958), *The Principles of Science: A Treatise on Logic and Scientific Method* [1907]. New York: Dover Publications.

Kerferd, G. B. (1981), *The Sophistic Movement*. Cambridge and New York: Cambridge University Press.

Keynes, John Maynard. (1936), *The General Theory of Employment Interest and Money*. New York and London: Harcourt Brace Jovanovich.

Khan, Rahat Nabi. (1988), "Science, Scientists, and Society: Public Attitudes towards Science and Technology", *Impact of Science on Society*, Vol. 38, No. 2, 257–271.

146   *Knowledge Without Expertise*

aphy">Koch, Donald F. (1984), *The Psychology of Moral Development: The Nature and Validity of Moral Stages*. San Francisco: Harper and Row.

———. (1986), "Moral Philosophers and Moral Expertise," *Philosophy and Medicine Newsletter* Fall:2–3.

Kohlberg, Lawrence. (1981), *The Meaning and Measurement of Moral Development*. Worcester, MA: Clark University Press.

Kohlstedt, Sally Gregory. (1976), *The Formation of the American Scientific Community: The American Association for the Advancement of Science 1848–1860*. Urbana, IL: University of Illinois Press.

Koot, Gerard M. (1980), "English Historical Economics and the Emergence of Economic History in England," *History of Political Economy*, 12:174–205.

Kuhn, Thomas S. (1970), *The Structure of Scientific Revolutions* [1962]. Chicago: University of Chicago Press.

Laski, Harold J. (1931), *The Limitations of the Expert*. London: The Fabian Society.

Latour, Bruno. (1987), *Science in Action: How to Follow Scientists and Engineers Through Society*. Cambridge: Harvard University Press.

———, and Steve Woolgar. (1986), *Laboratory Life: The Construction of Scientific Facts* [1979]. Princeton, NJ: Princeton University Press.

Levine, A. L. (1983), "Marshall's *Principles* and the "Biological Viewpoint: A Reconsideration," *The Manchester School of Economic and Social Studies*, LI:276–93.

Lieberman, Jethro K. (1970), *The Tyranny of the Experts: How Professionals are Closing the Open Society*. New York: Walker and Co.

Lifton, Robert Jay. (1986), *The Nazi Doctors: Medical Killing and the Psychology of Genocide*. New York: Basic Books.

Lindberg, David C. (1976), *Theories of Vision from Al-Kindi to Kepler*. Chicago: University of Chicago Press.

Locke, John. (1947), *Two Treatises of Government* [1690], ed. Thomas I. Cook. New York: Hafner Press.

Longino, Helen. (1990), *Science as Social Knowledge*. Princeton, NJ: Princeton University Press.

Lowry, Richard. (1971), *The Evolution of Psychological Theory*. Chicago: Aldine-Atherton.

Lyotard, Jean-François. (1984), *The Postmodern Condition: A Report on Knowledge* [1979], trans. by G. Bennington, and B. Massumi. Minneapolis: University of Minnesota Press.

————. (1988), *The Differend: Phrases in Dispute* [1983], trans. by G. Van Den Abbeele. Minneapolis: University of Minnesota Press.

————, and Jean-Loup Thebaud. (1985), *Just Gaming* [1979], trans. by W. Godzich. Minneapolis: University of Minnesota Press.

Machiavelli, Niccolo. (1977), "Discourses on the First Ten Books of Titus Livius," Norton Critical Edition of *The Prince*, trans. Robert M. Adams. New York: W. W. Norton.

MacKenzie, Donald A. (1981), *Statistics in Britain 1865–1930: The Social Construction of Scientific Knowledge*. Edinburgh: Edinburgh University Press.

Maloney, John. (1985), *Marshall, Orthodoxy and the Professionalisation of Economics*. Cambridge: Cambridge University Press.

Malthus, Thomas R. (1970), *An Essay on the Principle of Population* [1798], edited by Anthony Flew. Harmondsworth, England: Penguin Books.

148   *Knowledge Without Expertise*

Marshall, Alfred. (1885), "The Present Position of Economics," In *Memorials of Alfred Marshall*, edited by A. C. Pigou. London: Macmillan and Co., 1925.

———. (1898), "Mechanical and Biological Analogies in Economics," *Memorials of Alfred Marshall*. London: Macmillan and Co., 1925.

———. (1948), *Principles of Economics: An Introductory Volume* [1890]. 8th ed. New York: The Macmillan Company.

Marx, Karl. (1964), "Economic and Philosophical Manuscripts of 1844," In *Karl Marx: Early Writings* [1844], trans. and ed. by T. B. Bottomore. New York: McGraw-Hill.

———. (1978), *Capital: A Critique of Political Economy* [1887–1897]. Moscow: Progress Publishers.

Mazur, Allen. (1973), "Disputes Between Experts," *Minerva* 11, 243–263.

McCauley, Robert N. (1986), "Intertheoretical Relations and the Future of Psychology," *Philosophy of Science*, 53, 179–199.

Mill, John S. (1984), *On Liberty* [1859]. Harmondsworth, England: Penguin Books.

Morrell, Jack, and Arnold Thackray. (1981), *Gentlemen of Science: Early Years of the British Association for the Advancement of Science*. Oxford: Clarendon Press.

Morrow, Glenn R. (1928), "Adam Smith: Moralist and Philosopher," *Adam Smith, 1776–1926*; Lectures to Commemorate the Sesquicentennial of the Publication of "The Wealth of Nations," edited by John M. Clark, Paul H. Douglas, Jacob H. Hollander, Glenn R. Morrow, Melchior Polyi, and Jacob Viner. Chicago: University of Chicago Press.

Moss, Laurence. (1982), "Biological Theory and Technological Entrepreneurship in Marshall's Writings," *Eastern Economic Journal*, VIII:3–13.

Nelkin, Dorothy. (1975), "The Political Impact of Technical Expertise," *Social Studies of Science* 5:35–54.

Ormiston, Gayle L., and Raphael Sassower. (1989), *Narrative Experiments: The Discursive Authority of Science and Technology*. Minneapolis: University of Minnesota Press.

Pacey, Arnold. (1983), *The Culture of Technology*. Cambridge, MA: MIT Press.

Pearson, Karl. (1914/1924/1930), *The Life, Letters and Labours of Francis Galton*. Cambridge: Cambridge University Press.

———. (1922), *Francis Galton 1822–1922: A Centenary Appreciation*. London: Cambridge University Press.

Pockley, Peter. (1988), "Communicating Science to the Sceptics," *Impact of Science on Society*, Vol. 38, No. 2, 219–229.

Polanyi, Michael. (1958), *Personal Knowledge*. New York: Harper and Row.

———. (1964), *Science, Faith and Society* [1946]. Chicago and London: University of Chicago Press.

———. (1966), *The Tacit Dimension*. New York: Doubleday and Co.

Karl R. Popper. (1959), *The Logic of Scientific Discovery* [1935]. New York: Harper and Row.

———. (1968), *Conjectures and Refutations: The Growth of Scientific Knowledge* [1963]. New York: Harper and Row.

———. (1971), *The Open Society and Its Enemies* [1962], Vol. I, p. 4. Princeton: Princeton University Press.

———. (1979), *Objective Knowledge: An Evolutionary Approach* [1972]. Oxford: Oxford University Press.

Quesnay, Francois. (1969), *Tableau Économique des Physiocrates* [1758]. Paris: Calmann-Levy.

Radniztky, Gerard, and Peter Bernholz, eds. (1987), *Economic Imperialism: The Economic Method Applied Outside the Field of Economics*. New York: Paragon House Publishers.

Rankin, H. D. (1983), *Sophists, Socratics and Cynics*. London and Canberra: Croom Helm.

Redner, Harry. (1986), *The Ends of Philosophy*. Totowa, NJ: Rowman and Allanheld.

Reisman, D. A. (1976), *Adam Smith's Sociological Economics*. New York: Barnes and Noble Books.

Ricardo, David. (1911), *The Principles of Political Economy and Taxation* [1817]. London: J. M. Dent and Sons Ltd.

Robbins, Lionel. (1976), *Political Economy: Past and Present, A Review of Leading Theories of Economic Policy*. New York: Columbia University Press.

————. (1984), *An Essay on the Nature and Significance of Economic Science* [1932]. London: Macmillan.

Roberts, Marc J., Stephen R. Thomas, and Michael J. Dowling. (1984), "Mapping Scientific Disputes That Affect Public Policymaking," *Science, Technology, and Human Values*, 9:112–122.

Roll, Eric. (1953), *A History of Economic Thought*. 3rd ed. Englewood-Cliffs, NJ: Prentice Hall.

Rowe, C. J. (1983), "Plato on the Sophists as Teachers of Virtue," *History of Political Thought*, Vol. IV, No. 3, 400–427.

Russell, Bertrand. (1950), *Unpopular Essays*. New York: Simon and Schuster.

Sassower, Raphael. (1985), *Philosophy of Economics: A Critique of Demarcation*. Lanham, MD: University Press of America.

————. (1988a), "The Myth of Expertise," *Social Concept* 4:58–66.

————. (1988b), "Ideology Masked as Science: Shielding Economics from Criticism," *Journal of Economic Issues* XXII: 167–179.

————. (1989), "Critical Synthesis on the Interdisciplinary Relations Between Economics and Psychology: Estranged Bedfellows or Fellow Travellers?" *Social Epistemology* 3:269–280.

————. (1991a), "Therapeutic Moments in Technology Assessment," *Technology in Society* 12:441–455.

————. (1991b), "Scarcity and setting the boundaries of political economy," *Social Epistemology.* Vol. 4, No. 1, 75–91.

————, and Charla P. Ogaz. (1991), "Philosophical Hierarchies and Lyotard's Dichotomies," *Philosophy Today* 35:153–160.

Schumpeter, Joseph A. (1954), *History of economic Analysis*, edited by E. B. Schumpeter. Oxford: Oxford University Press.

Serres, Michel. (1982), *Hermes: Literature, Science, Philosophy*, eds. J. V. Harari, and D. F. Bell. Baltimore: Johns Hopkins University Press.

Shakespeare, William. "The Merchant of Venice," [1596/1600] In *The Works of William Shakespeare*. New York: Oxford University Press.

Shanahan, Timothy. (1990), "Evolution, Phenotypic Selection, and the Units of Selection," *Philosophy of Science*, Vol. 57, No. 2, 210–225.

Sidgwick, Henry. (1926), "Political Economy," *Palgrave's Dictionary of Political Economy*, ed. by Henry Higgs. London: Macmillan and Co.

Simon, Herbert. (1983), *Reason in Human Affairs*. Stanford: Stanford University Press.

de Sismondi, J. C. L. Simonde. (1966), *Political Economy* [1815]. New York: Augustus M. Kelley.

Skinner, Andrew S. (1979), *A System of Social Science: Papers Relating to Adam Smith*. Oxford: Clarendon Press.

————, and R. H. Campbell. (1982), *Adam Smith*. New York: St. Martin's Press.

Slayton, Philip, and Michael J. Trebilcock. (1978), *The Professions and Public Policy*. Toronto: University of Toronto Press.

Smith, Adam. (1937), *An Inquiry into the Nature and Causes of the Wealth of Nations* [1776], ed. by Edwin Cannan. New York: The Modern Library.

————. (1976), *The Theory of Moral Sentiments* [1759]. Indianapolis: Liberty Classics.

Smith, Kenneth. (1951), *The Malthusian Controversy*. London: Routledge and Kegan Paul.

Snow, C. P. (1986), *The Two Cultures and A Second Look* [1959]. Cambridge: Cambridge University Press.

Sperber, Irwin. (1990), *Fashions in Science: Opinion Leaders and Collective Behavior in the Social Sciences*. Minneapolis: University of Minnesota Press.

Stich, Stephen P., and Richard E. Nisbett. (1984), "Expertise, Justification, and the Psychology of Inductive Reasoning," *The Authority of Experts: Studies in History and Theory*. Bloomington, IN: Indiana University Press.

Stigler, George J. (1965), "The Influence of Events and Policies on Economic Theory," *Essays in the History of Economics*. Chicago and London: University of Chicago Press.

————. (1984), *The Intellectual and the Marketplace*. Cambridge, MA: Harvard University Press.

Szasz, Thomas S. (1974), *The Myth of Mental Illness: Foundations of a Theory of Personal Conduct*. New York: Harper and Row.

————. (1987), *Insanity: The Idea and its Consequences*. New York: John Wiley.

Todhunter, Isaac. (1865), *A History of the Mathematical Theory of Probability: From the Time of Pascal to that of Laplace*. Cambridge: Macmillan and Co.

Veblen, Thorstein. (1899), *The Theory of the Leisure Class: An Economic Study of Institutions*. New York: New American Library.

West, E. G. (1976), *Adam Smith: The Man and His Works*. Indianapolis: Liberty Press.

Wheeler, Raymond H. (1929), *The Science of Psychology*. New York: Thomas Crowell.

Whewell, William. (1862), *Six Lectures on Political Economy*. Cambridge: Cambridge University Press.

Wicksteed, Philip H. (1933), *The Common Sense of Political Economy and Selected Papers and Reviews on Economic Theory* [1910], ed. Lionel Robbins. London: Routledge and Kegan Paul Ltd.

Winch, Peter. (1958), *The Idea of a Social Science and its Relation to Philosophy*. London: Routledge and Kegan Paul.

————. (1964), "Understanding a Primitive Society," *American Philosophical Quarterly*, Vol. I, No. 4, 307–324.

Winner, Langdon. (1986), *The Whale and the Reactor: A Search for Limits in an Age of High Technology*. Chicago: University of Chicago Press.

Wittgenstein, Ludwig. (1969), *On Certainty*, trans. by D. Paul and G. E. M. Anscombe. New York: Harper and Row.

Yates, Frances A. (1964), *Giordano Bruno and the Hermetic Tradition*. Chicago: University of Chicago Press.

Young, S. David. (1987), *The Rule of Experts: Occupational Licensing in America*. Washington, D.C.: Cato Institute.

INDEX OF NAMES

Habermas, Jürgen, 101, 107–108
Hamlin, Christopher, 140
Hammond, Kenneth, 79-80, 87
Harcourt, William Vernon, 3, 6, 135
Harvey, William, 23
Hegel, 27, 60
Henderson, James, 136
Hey, John, 80
Hirshleifer, J., 25
Hofstadter, Richard, 19, 42, 111–112
Hollander, Samuel, 9
Howarth, O.J.R., 10–11, 16, 19–20
Hume, David, 89, 139
Huxley, Thomas Henry, 23

Ingram, J.K., 2–3, 19, 21–28, 135

Jevons, William, 26, 87, 139
Jones, Richard, 6, 135

Kerferd, G.B., 59–60
Khan, Rahat Nabi, 104
Kohlberg, Lawrence, 88
Kohlstedt, Sally G., 135–136, 138
Koot, Gerard M., 12, 27, 137
Kuhn, Thomas, 66, 80, 105–106

Laski, Harold, 109–113
Latour, Bruno, 66, 71
Levine, A.L., 25
Lewis, Alan, 79
Lieberman, Jethro, 140
Lindberg, David, 66
Locke, John, 95
Longino, Helen, 43
Lowry, Richard, 139
Lyotard, Jean-François, xiv, 49,
    53–58, 60–63, 67, 71–75,
    112–113

Machiavelli, 104, 110
MacKenzie, Donald, 137

Maloney, John, 18, 22, 27, 33, 137
Malthus, Thomas, 6, 32–34, 98–99
Marshall, Alfred, 2, 24–26, 136–137
Marx, Karl, 79, 85, 96–99, 119
Mason, Roger, 81
Mazur, Allan, 109
McCauley, Robert, 139
Menger, Carl, 79, 87–88, 139
Mill, John S., 108, 114, 139
Mills, John, 21
Morrell, Jack, 3–8, 10, 18, 135–136
Morrow, Glenn, 93
Moss, Laurence, 25
Mulkay, Michael, 140

Nelkin, Dorothy, 114–115, 140
Newton, 9, 105, 136
Nietzsche, Friedrich, 37, 50, 82, 120
Nightingale, Florence, 20
Nisbett, Richard, 140

Ormiston, Gayle, 49–50, 102
Owen, Robert, 10

Pacey, Arnold, 110
Pareto, Vilfredo, 79
Pearson, Karl, 17–18, 24, 137
Plato, 59, 69, 120, 138
Pockley, Peter, 104
Polanyi, Michael, 66, 105–106, 111
Popper, Karl, 52, 67, 82, 89, 105,
    107, 112, 119, 139
Price, Bonamy, 12–13
Ptolemy, 44

Quesnay, Francois, 23
Quetelet, Adolphe, 6

Radnitzky, Gerard, 86
Rankin, H.D., 59–60
Redner, Harry, 82
Reeve, Colin, 6

155

Reisman, D.A., 93
Ricardo, David, 2, 9, 136
Robbins, Lionel, 89–90
Roll, Eric, 88
Rousseau, Jean-Jacques, x
Rowe, C.J., 59
Russell, Bertrand, 112–113, 140
Rutherford, Malcolm, 138

Schumpeter, Joseph, 73, 87–88, 139
Sedgwick, Adam, 6–7
Senior, Nassau William, 34
Serres, Michel, 48
Shakespeare, William, 30, 34–36
Skinner, Andrew, 93–94
Shanahan, Timothy, 41
Simon, Herbert, 80
Slovic, Paul, 80
Smith, Adam, 2, 9, 23–25, 79, 81,
    85, 89, 91–95, 97–99, 139
Snow, C.P., 110
Socrates, xiv, 35, 37, 48, 59–60, 65,
    67–68, 72, 120
Spencer, Herbert, 24
Sperber, Irwin, 115
Spinoza, 29, 38, 128
Spottiswoode, William, 13
Stich, Stephen, 140
Stigler, George, 94–95, 106–108,
    110, 139–140
Szasz, Thomas, 86, 140

Thackery, Arnold, 3–8, 10, 18, 83,
    135–136
Thebaud, Jean-Loup, 49, 55–56,
    61–63
Thomson, Allen, 13
Todhunter, Isaac, 79
Toynbee, Arnold, 12

Veblen, Thorstein, 81

Weber, Max, 36, 79, 107
West, E.G., 94
Wheeler, Raymond, 139
Whewell, William, 2–3, 6–12, 18–22,
    30, 135–136
Wicksteed, Philip, 83, 87–89, 138
Winch, Peter, 40, 43–44
Winner, Langdon, 111
Wittgenstein, Ludwig, 43, 70, 74–75
Woolgar, Steve, 66

Yates, Frances, 45–47
Young, David, 140

INDEX OF SUBJECTS

157